"We all have fears as we raise our children, and we try so hard to get it right, though we're never quite certain if we are where we should be. Ken Barish, who has been there as a parent and has seen almost everything kids can get into during his years of practice, provides the information you seek and helps you get your bearings. If you are a parent, you will reach for this book like it's the hand of a dear and knowing friend reaching out to offer help. *Pride and Joy* is a superb book—brilliant, wise, timely, and fun to read. It is heartfelt and full of treasures every parent will store up and use."—Edward (Ned) Hallowell, M.D., Founder of The Hallowell Center for Cognitive and Emotional Health and author of *The Childhood Roots of Adult Happiness*

"This is a wonderful book! This practical and very wise book will support parents and guardians thinking about how to best manage the struggles that all children—and all families—have. I wish that I had been able to read this book when I became a father."—Jonathan Cohen, Ph.D., President, Center for Social and Emotional Education and Adjunct Professor in Psychology and Education, Teachers College, Columbia University

"Stepping into the national debate over whether parents are too soft, or too worried, or too distracted to raise strong kids, Dr. Barish shares his insights into the emotional lives of children and what kids need from parents to develop resilience, optimism, the capacity for hard work, and the other good things we want for them. Dr. Barish understands that parenting can be child-centered without indulging or catering to children. By acknowledging kids' feelings, we can more effectively help them develop self-discipline. He offers an excellent guide to building the kind of warm, positive relationship with kids that is the key to setting, and enforcing, the limits that they need."—Harold S. Koplewicz, M.D., President, Child Mind Institute

"Compassionate, respectful, and inspiring. This book stands out from the crowded field of parenting books."—Ellen F. Wachtel, Ph.D., author of *Treating Troubled Children and Their Families*

"*Pride and Joy* is a book overflowing with the unmistakable signs of wisdom that only decades of experience can produce." —Marshall P. Duke, Ph.D., Charles Howard Candler Professor of Psychology, Emory University and Editor of *Journal of Family Life*

"Understanding children requires understanding and responding wisely to the emotions that enliven—and sometimes undermine—children's everyday experience. Dr. Barish expertly weaves together the insights of developmental science, a clinician's experience, and the practical knowledge of a father to provide guidance to the challenges of parenthood. This book is wise and smart."—Ross A. Thompson, Ph.D., Distinguished Professor, Department of Psychology, University of California–Davis

"Written in an accessible manner, Dr. Barish offers many nuggets of advice concerning the rearing of children in this confusing, complex society. He emphasizes the need to support children's emotional health through sharing their joys, offering solace when they are sad or disappointed, and by addressing any conflicts that may occur between parent and child. Research is cited throughout the book, but in language that is lucid and free of jargon. Dr. Barish cites many examples that deal with children's problems drawn from his clinical practice, adding to the richness of this book."—Dr. Dorothy G. Singer, Department of Psychology, Yale University

PRIDE AND JOY

PRIDE AND JOY

A Guide to Understanding Your Child's Emotions and Solving Family Problems

Kenneth Barish, Ph.D.

OXFORD
UNIVERSITY PRESS

OXFORD
UNIVERSITY PRESS

Oxford University Press, Inc., publishes works that further
Oxford University's objective of excellence
in research, scholarship, and education.

Oxford New York
Auckland Cape Town Dar es Salaam Hong Kong Karachi
Kuala Lumpur Madrid Melbourne Mexico City Nairobi
New Delhi Shanghai Taipei Toronto

With offices in
Argentina Austria Brazil Chile Czech Republic France Greece
Guatemala Hungary Italy Japan Poland Portugal Singapore
South Korea Switzerland Thailand Turkey Ukraine Vietnam

Published by Oxford University Press, Inc.
198 Madison Avenue, New York, New York 10016
www.oup.com

Library of Congress Cataloging-in-Publication Data

Barish, Kenneth.
Pride and joy : a guide to understanding your child's emotions and
solving family problems / Kenneth Barish.
p. cm.
Includes bibliographical references and index.
ISBN 978-0-19-989624-0 (pbk.)
1. Emotions in children. 2. Parent and child. 3. Parenting. I. Title.
BF723.E6B25 2012
155.4'124—dc23 2011040999

9 8 7 6 5
Printed in the United States of America
on acid-free paper

This book is dedicated

with all my love

to my family—to Harriet, Rachel, Dan, and now Alex.

CONTENTS

PART II: Solving Common Problems of Family Life

PART III: Conclusion

ACKNOWLEDGMENTS

So many people have helped me write this book.

I want to express my appreciation to the friends, colleagues, and family members who generously gave their time and effort to read earlier versions of the book, and offered helpful criticism.

Thank you to Dan Barish, Harriet Barish, Jenny Barish, Steve Barish, Laura Bartels, Judy Berenson, Diane Caspe, Bob Congdon, Mary Beth Congdon, Rand Gruen, Lisa Lipman, Edie Mencher, Arnold Richards, Jean Schreiber, Tom Schreiber, Jeff Silberman, Don Sklansky, Rachel Barish Swartz, Joan Tapper, John Turtz, Arnold Zinman, and four anonymous reviewers.

I owe a very special debt of gratitude to Sarah Harrington, my editor at OUP, for her willingness to support this project and for her careful readings of the manuscript at all stages of its development. Every aspect of this book—its content, organization, and style—has benefited from Sarah's thoughtful and wise advice.

I could not write any book without the help of Marcia Miller, librarian of New York-Presbyterian Hospital, Westchester Division, and without the help of my secretary, Bobbie Gallagher.

I would also like to express my appreciation to the faculties of the Westchester Center for the Study of Psychoanalysis and Psychotherapy, the William Alanson White Institute Child and

Adolescent Psychotherapy Training Program, and the Department of Psychiatry, Weill Medical College, for offering me the opportunity to teach—and learn from—engaging and talented students.

And a special thank you, as always, to my friend Mary Caldwell, for more than 60 years of friendship and support to four generations of the Barish family.

My parents, Min and Bernie Barish, are, sadly, no longer with us. Their love and their generosity, however, remain a source of inspiration in the lives of their children and grandchildren.

INTRODUCTION

Parenthood begins with one of life's most joyful moments.

Sadly, for many families, our joy too quickly fades. As we struggle to cope with the demands of being parents, with our uncertainty and stress, moments of joyfulness and pride in our children, although no less cherished, too often give way to argument, defiance, and withdrawal.

In this book, I hope to offer some guidance about how we can preserve and strengthen some of the joyfulness and pride that has been lost or eroded in our relationships with our children, and how we can foster our children's optimism and resilience in the face of life's inevitable disappointments.

For me, this is what being a parent is all about.

Several years ago, Mr. and Mrs. B consulted me about their 6-year-old daughter, Julia. During the past year, the life of this young family had been complicated by serious medical difficulties and economic stress. Now, when Julia came home from school, at the first disappointment of the afternoon, as soon as either of her parents was unable to provide her with undivided attention, Julia began to scream—insistent, relentless screaming.

Julia's screaming had reduced her intelligent and thoughtful parents to tears. Mr. and Mrs. B had lost patience with their daughter; their statements and tone with her had become increasingly harsh and punitive. Nothing had helped—ignoring her cries, offering rewards, or imposing "time-out" or more severe punishments. Mr. and Mrs. B sensed that these efforts had only made the situation worse, and they began to doubt their competence as parents.

I suggested to Julia's parents that they enlist Julia in the solution of this problem: to ask her that evening, in a calm moment, perhaps as they were putting her to bed, to tell them about the things that upset her, during the school day and at home. And then, to ask Julia for her ideas—what her parents could say or do to help her when she was upset. This way of talking with children is almost always helpful, even when the solutions kids offer are wildly unrealistic or unacceptable. Julia's parents were able to encourage their daughter, at least for that moment, to think differently—not about making a protest or a demand, but about how to solve an emotional problem.

But I did not anticipate the profound nature of Julia's answer. Julia did not say, "Give me more attention" or "Buy me a toy." Instead, she told her parents, "Tell me there will be a next time."

Julia's parents accepted their daughter's very reasonable suggestion. They began to help Julia anticipate and preview other times when she might begin to feel anxious or angry; they talked together about what Julia could do when her parents were not immediately available to help or comfort her; and they planned special activities that Julia could look forward to, writing them on the calendar. In this way, Julia learned to manage moments of frustration and disappointment. Her emotional crises soon ended and a family atmosphere of escalating anger and defiance gave way to renewed playfulness and emotional support. Julia also seemed to "internalize" these discussions; when Mrs. B was upset, Julia would console her, "Mommy, it's okay, tomorrow you'll feel better."

So often, families get stuck. Despite our best intentions, our children have become stubborn and defensive—and so have we. Parenting has become a chore, and our relationships with our children have been taken over by criticism and nagging. We may no longer spank, but we now yell.[1] Too many young parents today feel that being a parent does not bring greater happiness to their daily lives.[2]

Too many young parents today feel that being a parent does not bring greater happiness to their daily lives.

There are answers to these problems.

In this book, I will describe lessons I have learned over the course of three decades of talking with children and parents, listening to their concerns, and seeking practical solutions to the daily problems that trouble many contemporary families. I will also discuss lessons learned from colleagues engaged in clinical, developmental, and neuroscience research, and from my experience as a parent of two (now adult) children.

I will offer advice about how we can nurture our children's emotional health, how we can promote our children's social and character development, and how we can ameliorate the conflicts and arguments that are a source of distress to so many thoughtful and caring parents.

Images of Our Children's Futures

Being a parent, of course, is not only a source of great joy. It is also a source of our most sober—and sobering—responsibilities, and a test of our character. Our children will challenge us.

Children who are impulsive and strong willed will test the limits of our own emotional maturity.

We accept, as parents, a fundamental responsibility: to provide our children with both a practical and a moral education. We attempt to instill in our children those qualities of character (virtues) that have become important to us—to promote, by instruction and by example, the skills and moral values we believe they will need to take their place in adult society and to thrive as adults.

We are guided in this effort by an image of our child's future—an image of the kind of person we want our child to become. We are also influenced by a negative image—an image of the kind of person we *don't* want our child to become. These images shape our child-rearing philosophies and the daily decisions we make about our children's lives.

More Burdened and More Alone

Raising children in contemporary American society may be more emotionally difficult than at other times and other places. Because of the diffusion and breakdown of extended family networks and other social supports, modern parents have less help available to them, help that was once much more available to parents, as they attempt to cope with the demands and uncertainties all parents face in caring for their children. We are now more burdened and more alone. We are likely to live farther from our own parents, and we are less likely to know our neighbors.[3] Both parents and children now have fewer places to turn when they are in need of emotional and practical support.[4]

We are also less familiar with the world our children will live in as adults. We may have less control over the dangers, temptations, and destructive influences they will encounter than our parents did when we were growing up. We want our children to become competent, responsible, and caring adults. We are less certain, however, how to get them there.

Modern Parenting Advice: A Criticism

There is already much advice, and much good advice, available to parents about raising emotionally healthy children—children who are optimistic and resilient, and who engage in life with a sense of purpose. For decades there has been good advice available about how to reduce conflict with our children, and good advice is increasingly available on coping with the challenges of raising children with difficult temperaments.

Most advice offered to parents, however, continues to focus less on understanding our children's *emotions* and more on managing a child's problematic *behavior*. Parents are taught, often in scientifically tested programs, how to "shape" cooperative behavior, how to impose effective penalties when children misbehave, even how long to wait for a child to obey before imposing a consequence or time-out—all with the goal of achieving improved compliance with parental demands. This advice is offered in the form of tools and skills that will help us become more "effective" parents. The parenting "skills" approach seems to largely define our current parenting philosophy.

These skills are undoubtedly helpful to many parents. Better methods for setting limits and eliciting children's cooperation with basic tasks help reduce daily conflicts with our children and introduce needed structure into family life. Increased cooperation relieves parents of frequent frustration and resentment, allowing them to then engage more positively in other ways with their children—and with each other.

Over time, I have therefore come to appreciate the value of an effectiveness approach to parenting.[5] But these methods also have limitations.

I like to think of the word *parent* as a noun—before it is a verb. Our character as parents, in the long run, is certainly more important than our parenting "techniques." Spending more time playing and talking with our children, understanding their anxieties, frustrations, and concerns, and creating moments of encouragement and joy are more important to being a parent—and to our children's emotional health—than counting to three when they don't listen or learning the right words to use when stating a command.

Our character as parents is certainly more important than our parenting "techniques."

Even in the best advice offered, advice on strengthening family relationships, on improving communication and understanding between parents and children, on sharing and having fun together, I often find something missing, something that goes to the heart of being a parent. We do not stop often enough, I believe, to consider our idealization in the eyes of our children—how children look to us and look up to us—and how we remain for our children, throughout life, sources of affirmation and emotional support.

In *Wisdom of Our Fathers*, Tim Russert's collection of the correspondence he received following the publication of his memoir of his relationship with his own father, Russert includes this letter from Beth Hackett, daughter of Roger Hackett:

> I was an only child. Mom said I was plenty; Dad said I was perfect. He worked hard to support us: twelve-hour shifts with thirteen days on and only one day off, because

> overtime paid the bills. He left early in the morning, long before mom and I were awake. He came home exhausted and slept until it was time to do it all over again. It was hard on him because he had so little time with us. It was hard on us too.
>
> We all found little ways to compensate. Mom would pack his lunch and take one bite of his sandwich, so he would smile when it was time to eat. I would put my favorite toy in his lunch box so he had something to play with at lunch.
>
> Dad's special time with me was morning coffee. He would get up at 4:00 AM, start the coffee brewing, and get ready for work. When the pot was ready, he would come into my room and wake me up. I would sit at the kitchen table as he poured two cups of coffee. His was always black. Mine was barely brown, full of milk and sugar, sweet to the taste. Dad would tell me about his day and ask about mine. When the cups were empty, he would tuck me back into bed and kiss me good night before heading out to work. It was our special time together, and we never missed. . . .
>
> He died in 1995, and I still miss him. Every morning I make a pot of coffee and sit at the kitchen table. . . . When I raise my mug, . . . I see my dad sitting across from me, a smile on his face and a cup of coffee in his hands . . . . It's always special. I'm having coffee with my dad.[6]

I found in this moving story something of the essence of being a parent. Mr. Hackett's parenting was not based on a technique or skill that can be taught or trained. It was a creative, generous expression of empathy and love, inspired by a father's desire to create moments of pleasure and sharing with his daughter, and to make this his priority, despite the demands of his work. And Mr. Hackett's love, in return, evoked in his daughter a lifelong feeling of love and gratitude.

Ms. Hacket may have been, as her mother said, "plenty." She may even have been a handful. She will face difficulties in her life, as we all do, and the memory of her father's love will not solve these problems. But she has learned from her parents, in a profound way, how to care about the needs and feelings of others, a life lesson certainly as important as any other. When she misbehaves, as all children do, and her father needs to assert his authority, he will be a respected authority (even if she does not always listen). She will have with her, in moments of sadness and loneliness, in childhood and in her adult life, a deep and indelible feeling of inner support. And she will continue to look up to him.[7]

Plan of the Book

The central theme and message of this book is the importance of understanding our children's emotions. Emotions, we now know, are not just feelings. In childhood, and throughout life, our emotions guide our thoughts and our imagination, our behavior, and our moral judgments.

A deeper appreciation of children's emotions can offer parents better solutions to the problems in their lives.

I will attempt to show how a deeper appreciation of the full range of children's emotions—their positive emotions of interest, joy, and pride as well as their painful feelings of sadness, anxiety, anger, and shame—can offer parents new perspectives on their children's development—and better solutions to the problems in their lives.

In Part I, I summarize some basic principles of emotional health and positive character development. I discuss seven essential emotions of childhood and explain why they are important in the life of a developing child. I present my understanding as a child therapist, supported by scientific research, of healthy and unhealthy emotional development—what goes right and what goes wrong in the lives of healthy and troubled children and families. I then describe the principles of Positiveness and Repair, and how we can best nurture our children's social and moral development. These chapters offer advice on how, as parents, we can help children bounce back from discouragement and disappointment, repair family relationships that have been damaged by frequent anger and resentment, and preserve our children's idealism and their concern for others.

Part II addresses problems of daily family life—rules and limits, doing homework and going to sleep, winning and losing at games, our children's reluctance to talk to us, their tantrums and lack of motivation, and their addiction to television and video games. In these chapters I offer recommendations for solving these common but often difficult problems.

Then, in a concluding chapter, I review the essential messages of the book. I present a personal philosophy and final take-away advice, a summary of lessons learned—lessons about being a parent and what matters most to our children's happiness and their success in life.

The recommendations I will offer are drawn from many traditions and sources of knowledge. We can find wisdom—and helpful advice—about raising our children in many places. In our efforts to help our children and our families, parents (and therapists) need all the help that we can get.

In the course of the book, I will also engage many of the controversies of contemporary parenting: Have we created a "culture of indulgence" that is harmful to our society and to our children?

Are we overprotective and oversolicitous? Are our children overpraised? How can we balance our concern for our children's *achievement* with their responsibilities as *citizens*? How can we strengthen their sense of purpose and their commitment to ideals? How can we provide our children with effective guidance and discipline when children, as they inevitably will, misbehave? In these discussions, I will be fair but not shy. I will give careful and respectful consideration to the opinions of others and then offer my own opinions and judgments.

Some Essential Clarifications

In presenting advice on strengthening children's emotional health, it is important for me to make clear, from the outset, some fundamental facts about children's personalities and about emotional and behavioral problems in childhood.

Children begin life with unique, and sometimes difficult, temperaments. They may be anxious and shy, or impulsive, inattentive, and strong willed. These traits of temperament, along with other biological vulnerabilities (for example, a child's vulnerability to depression) are important in the development of many, perhaps most, psychological and behavioral problems of childhood. Parents should also know that psychiatric medicine is often helpful in the treatment of these problems. The era of blaming parents for all of children's emotional problems is, thankfully, past. Nature is important. But, of course, nurture is important, too.

I am often asked a critical question: "When should I seek professional help for my child?" I would offer this general advice: If you feel that you are stuck in your family relationships, if your child is unhappy or having difficulty making friends, or if he says that he hates school, there is no reason to wait. I have seen too many families wait too long, when some simple professional advice or an early evaluation could have made things much better, much sooner, and the vicious cycles of unhealthy family interactions I will describe in this book could have been prevented. Child therapists now have a broad range of options available to help children and families. A brief consultation, as in the case of Julia, is often very helpful.

Scope and Limits

This book will focus on the emotional development of children from preschool age through early adolescence. I will not offer recommendations for problems of infancy and toddlerhood, for example, problems of early attachment, feeding, and toilet training. These problems are beyond the range of my clinical expertise. Adolescence also brings its own special set of challenges, for both parents and therapists, that warrant a separate discussion.

I will not offer opinions about what is happening in our nation's schools; educational policies and practices are, again, outside my area of expertise. I am also not an expert on broader parenting trends, a topic of significant controversy. Advocates of firm discipline believe that we have created a culture of permissiveness and indulgence, and cite evidence to support this conclusion. Advocates of a more child-centered approach also cite evidence—that harsh punishment and controlling methods of child rearing, frequent criticizing and yelling, continue to be pervasive problems in contemporary families. Perhaps both sides are right. On this issue, I can only speak authoritatively of my own clinical and personal experience.

Finally, although many parents will welcome my recommendations, I am aware that others will remain skeptical. To some parents (and to some of my colleagues) my focus on children's emotions (and only secondarily on their behavior), my willingness to compromise (in an effort to teach compromise) and to engage children in active problem solving (in order to teach problem solving) may seem to be the wrong lessons, too much "giving in" to a child's demands—at odds, in some important respect, with their parenting philosophy.

I hope, however, that even skeptical readers will find some new perspectives in the understanding and advice that I offer; some help in improving their relationships with their children; and some solutions to the repetitive and disheartening conflicts that, too often, undermine the happiness of our children—and our own pleasure in being parents.

PART I

Basic Principles

Nurturing Your Child's Emotional Health

Chapter 1

The Emotions of Childhood

Joyousness and wonder are the characteristic emotions of childhood.

—THOMAS COLE

When talking about children's emotions, it is often difficult to avoid saying things that are not already commonly known, or even common sense. Recent advances in the psychology and neuroscience of emotions, however, now offer us a new understanding of the nature of emotion—and of the importance of emotion—in our own lives and in the lives of our children.

Emotions are not just feelings. Emotions focus our attention, direct our thoughts and our imagination, evoke memories, and prepare us for action. Emotions are signals, to others and to ourselves, evoked by "concerns." Every emotion brings about changes, not only in how we feel but also in our physiology and motivation, our thoughts and our behavior.

In this chapter I will discuss seven important emotions of childhood and offer some thoughts about the essential role of these emotions in our children's emotional health.

Interest

Nineteenth-century American landscape painter Thomas Cole included the statement at the beginning of this chapter as an annotation to his famous series of paintings, *The Voyage of Life*.[1] Cole was right. Understanding children begins with a child's sense of awe and wonder, and feelings of joy. Curiosity and wonder, so evident in the enthusiasms of young children and so much a part of their charm, are expressions of the basic human emotion of *interest*.

Many of us may not, at first, think of interest as an emotion. Psychologists and neuroscientists, however, now regard interest as a fundamental emotion—an emotion that motivates and guides our engagement in the world.[2] Without interest, there is no curiosity, no exploration, and no real learning. Interest is therefore an essential part of what all parents want for their children: the ability to sustain effort toward future goals.

Interest is vital to emotional health in childhood, and it remains vital, throughout life. The philosopher Bertrand Russell considered our continued interest in and enjoyment of many things—a quality he called "zest"—to be "the most universal and distinctive mark of happy men." Russell correctly observed that "young children are interested in everything that they see and hear." He added that "genuine zest is part of the natural order of things" and "a feeling of being loved promotes zest more than anything else."[3] Modern scientific research has confirmed Russell's philosophic insights.

Interest may be a child's first emotion. Infants show intense interest in their mothers' faces, especially her eyes.[4] Soon, children become interested in objects that are colorful, moving, rhythmic, or harmonious (or, more generally, beautiful). And young children are wide eyed in their curiosity and interest in the lives of their parents.

Interest is also of critical importance to our relationships with our children. As parents, our enthusiastic responsiveness to our children's interests is the surest way to engage them in some form of meaningful dialogue or interaction, and a first principle of strengthening family relationships.

Interest and Motivation

Children express interest—or lack of interest—in different activities for the same reasons that we do, as adults. Like all of us, children want to do what makes them feel good, what they are "good at." For a child who is interested in music (or in art, literature, or athletics), the sounds that she hears (or images, words, or movements) evoke other sounds and other images, and "light up" the child's brain.[5]

Especially in early childhood, children want to do what *we* do—to be like those they admire. A child's interest is *sustained*, however (and ours is as well), by her feeling of progress toward reaching a goal and her expectation of eventual success.

> **As parents, our enthusiastic responsiveness to our children's interests is the surest way to engage them in dialogue, and a first principle of strengthening family relationships.**

Many parents express concern about the limited range of their child's interests and about their child's inability to sustain interest (and effort) toward important goals. As a therapist, I am often told, for example, "He's not *interested* in reading (or writing, or drawing, or riding a bicycle)." These parents experience frustration and dismay at their unsuccessful efforts to encourage, by any means—with any form of cajoling, rewards, or punishment—an expansion of their child's interests.

As with all emotional and behavioral problems of childhood, a child's temperament plays an important role in determining his interests and must always be considered in evaluating these concerns. Children differ in the nature of their interests. In most instances, however, when children say that they are not interested—when a child tells his parents, for example, that his schoolwork is "boring"—we may reasonably suspect that some other painful feeling, perhaps anxiety or lack of confidence, has restricted the range of the child's interests. His lack of interest (and lack of effort) is the result of his frustration (and perhaps also a feeling of shame), which leads first to discouragement and then to avoidance. When a child is not interested in reading, it is likely that learning to read does not come easily. His lack of *interest* in reading is the result of his *frustration* in learning to read, and he expresses his frustration through avoidance and protest.

Finally, interest, like every emotion, evokes imagination and fantasy. In childhood, these are especially fantasies of what he will be able to do or become, to be like the people he admires—perhaps a policeman, a baseball player, or an actor. Our appreciation of these common fantasies of childhood is another way to convey to children our understanding of what is important to them, their hopes and aspirations.

Joy

If interest is the first emotion of childhood, joy is our first emotion as parents.

The psychoanalyst Sandra Buechler has written that our capacity to experience joy requires a willingness to "love life anyway," despite sadness and regret. Joy evokes in us a feeling of sufficiency—a feeling that "I have everything I need."

Buechler explains that joy is more than pleasure and excitement. "Joy differs from pleasure and excitement in the time frame of the mark it leaves. Pleasure and excitement are wonderful moments now. But joy speaks . . . of how deeply satisfying life can be now and in the future."[6] Buechler also believes that joy is the "universal antidote" for all our painful emotions. We now have scientific evidence to support this belief.

The importance of joy for our emotional and physical health has been demonstrated in recent research. In a ground-breaking study, researchers found that joyful feeling expressed early in adult life, in the novitiate essays of young nuns, was remarkably predictive of these women's future health and longevity.[7] In presenting the results of the Harvard Study of Adult Development, George Vaillant observed that a capacity to experience joy, to maintain what one participant called a "celebrant sense" of life, was perhaps the most important component of successful aging. Vaillant tells his readers, "Whenever . . . I write pedantically of *successful aging*—think *joy*" (italics in original).[8]

Moments of mutual joy and delight between parents and infants are not only beneficial to our psychological health. They also have an important biological function. Neuroscientist Allan Schore has proposed that these moments—parent–infant interactions that generate high levels of shared interest and joyful feeling—directly promote brain development, especially the growth of pathways between limbic (emotional) and cortical (reasoning and problem-solving) areas of the brain.[9]

Moments of mutual joy and delight between parents and infants may directly promote brain development.

Joyful responsiveness is a first principle of child development. Your child's expectation of a joyful, affirming response—your delight in each new developmental milestone—has an important role in sustaining her (as all of us are sustained, throughout life) in the face of the inevitable frustrations and disappointments of growing up.

Joyfulness builds resilience and immunity.[10]

Pride and Shame

Discussions of children's motivations and behavior too often overlook the importance of feelings of pride and shame. A child's need to feel proud—and to avoid feelings of shame—is a fundamental motivation, and remains fundamental, throughout her life. It would be difficult to overestimate the importance of these emotions in the psychological development—and emotional health—of our children.[11]

Shame is our instinctive response to personal failure or inadequacy, especially the public exposure of inadequacy. Embarrassment is a temporary and mild form of shame; humiliation, aloneness, and self-hatred are severe forms of shame.[12]

Children experience feelings of shame when they suffer any social rejection; when they are unable to learn; when they are defeated in competition; when they are bullied, insulted, or taunted; and when they seek acceptance and approval from admired adults but are, instead, subjected to criticism or derogation.[13] When children tell us that they are anxious, they are often anxious about the possibility of feeling ashamed.

Children with difficulties in motor coordination or delays in language development experience shame early in childhood. Somewhat later, difficulties in learning, especially in learning to read, always evoke in children a deep feeling of shame. In childhood, shame leads to avoidance and withdrawal and then, in adolescence, to desperate attempts to alleviate, or get rid of, this painful state of mind. Many experiences that evoke a feeling of shame (for example, experiences of exclusion or ridicule) are uniquely painful, and the feeling of shame, perhaps more than any other emotion, stays with us.

I can still recall, more vividly and poignantly than I would like, moments of shame from many years ago when, as a son (and as a father), I let my parents (and my children) down. Although I have long since been forgiven for these personal failures, my memories are still painful. Thankfully, I am able to put these moments in perspective; they are now more than balanced by moments of pride. In this way, we should also help our children put in perspective their own moments of embarrassment and failure.

The shame and pride family of emotions may be our most recent, and most uniquely human, emotions. The emotions of pride and shame seem to be derived from instinctive expressions of social status—winning and losing, for example, in competitive encounters. Pride evolved from expressions of dominance—and still involves displays of dominance. The unabashed triumphant bragging of young boys and the more (or less) socialized exhibitionistic displays of victorious adult males (and the bragging of parents and grandparents about the accomplishments of their offspring) are instinctive expressions of pride. Shame, in contrast, originated as a signal of submission, saving the loser from further aggression and eliciting social support.[14]

When children are successful and feel proud, they instinctively look to others. When they fail and feel ashamed, they look away.[15] This is in the nature of pride and shame. The universal behavior associated with the emotion of shame is *concealment*; we all attempt to hide or cover up what we are ashamed of. Pride is the antithesis of shame. The feeling of pride is accompanied by an *outward* movement and a desire to show and tell others, to exhibit or show off. Pride is *expansive*, both in action and in our imagination. Shame *contracts*, in our posture (our shoulders fall in and we look downward and away) and in our thoughts and imagination—in our setting of goals and in what we consider possible for ourselves.

A child's expectation of feeling proud or ashamed therefore decisively influences her choices—those situations she actively seeks and those she avoids. Shame—our emotional response to exclusion and failure—lowers aspirations. Pride—our emotional response to acceptance and success—raises aspirations. The evolutionary psychologist Glenn Weisfeld succinctly explains, "We anticipate pride and shame at every turn and shape our behavior accordingly."[16]

Especially, children want their parents to share in their pride and to be proud of them. Our children's feeling—their inner certainty—that we are proud of them is an essential good feeling, an anchor that sustains them in moments of discouragement, aloneness, and defeat. Our feeling that our parents are proud of us is a motivating and sustaining force throughout our lives, and a protective factor in the emotional lives of our children. The opposite is also true. Parental scorn is among the most deeply destructive forces in the psychological development of any child.

Our children's inner certainty that we are proud of them sustains them in moments of discouragement, aloneness, and defeat.

When, as parents, we fail to express pride in our children, when we are frequently dismissive, critical, or disapproving, our children will be more vulnerable to emotional and behavioral problems of all kinds. They will live, more than they should, with discouragement and resentment. These feelings will then come to be expressed in some way, perhaps as defiance and rebellion, or as a failure of initiative, or as an inability to sustain effort toward long-term goals.

We need to let our children know, as often as we can, that we are proud of them—for their effort *and* for their accomplishments. And we should not be afraid to "spoil" them with this form of praise.

But why should we regard pride as a healthy emotion? Isn't pride too close to narcissism, an inflated sense of our own importance, "the deadliest of the seven deadly sins?"[17] Some parent advisors have raised just this concern—that parental indulgence has led to excessive pride in our children.

The solution to this apparent paradox, however, is not difficult. Emotion theorists now distinguish "authentic" pride—based on effort and actual accomplishment—from "hubristic" pride—based on feelings of superiority and a distorted, aggrandized self-image. Hubristic pride, as we have long known, is a defensive effort to cover up unacknowledged feelings of shame. We feel authentic pride because of what we *do*; we feel hubristic pride for who we *are* (or believe ourselves to be). Authentic pride is associated with positive social behavior. Hubristic pride is associated with arrogance and narcissism.[18]

Are Our Children Overpraised?

It has become common in recent years for parents to be warned about the dangers of praise. We are told that frequent praise, although intended to bolster a child's self-confidence and self-esteem, may instead create increased anxiety and ultimately undermine her initiative and confidence. Many parent advisors are especially concerned, even appalled, by empty praise—when parents (or teachers) tell children that they are wonderful (or worse, "special") when a child has not, in fact, done anything wonderful or special.

In this view, when praise is cheap, children fail to learn the importance of hard work. The critics ask, how can children learn the need for effort and perseverance when they are not challenged to do better, when they are given A's for C work, awarded trophies for just showing up, and only hear good things?[19]

My own experience—and, I believe, a correct reading of the research on praise—teaches a different lesson. In three decades of clinical practice, I have met many discouraged, angry, and unhappy children. I have met demoralized kids who were unable to sustain effort when they encountered even mild frustration or disappointment, and others who had developed attitudes of entitlement. And the culprit is not praise, but criticism. Most of these children were overcriticized; very few were overpraised.

Children need praise. We all do. From early in life, children look to us for praise and approval, and to share moments of pride. Of course, I do not recommend praise (or, for that matter, expressions of sympathy or solace) that is unrealistic or insincere. I certainly do not believe in empty praise.

But I believe that we should be generous, not stingy, with our praise.

A Growth Mindset

Psychologist Carol Dweck and her colleagues have conducted important research that demonstrates significant negative effects of praising children's *abilities*, rather than their *effort*. These studies have also shown important positive effects when children were taught that effort, not innate ability, was the key to success.[20] Dweck distinguishes two types of beliefs, or mindsets, that children (and adults) hold about the nature of our abilities. Children with a *fixed mindset* regard abilities, including intelligence, as unchangeable traits. Children with a *growth mindset* believe that our abilities can improve with effort.

When children have a fixed mindset, every challenge presented to them feels as if it were a test—a test of whether they are smart or not smart, talented or not talented. A fixed mindset creates a feeling of anxiety and urgency, and an inclination to avoid, rather than seek, risks and challenges. When stressed, children with a fixed mindset are more likely to feel anxious and depressed. They are also more likely to become defensive, to cheat, and to lie.[21] In contrast, when children have a growth mindset, they are more likely to regard their failures not as a judgment but as an opportunity for learning. Children with a growth mindset therefore show more optimism and persistence when faced with setbacks.

Praising children's intelligence fosters a fixed mindset. Praising children's effort promotes a growth mindset. Dweck and her colleagues have also shown, in both colleges and in junior high schools, that changing students' mindsets enhances their effort, their achievement, and their ability to respond adaptively to stress.[22]

Dweck concludes that "Praising children's intelligence harms their motivation and harms their performance." (She notes, of course, that children love this kind of praise. They love to be told that they are smart, and this gives them a boost, a special glow—but only for the moment.) Dweck does *not* conclude from this research, however, that parents should not praise their children. She writes,

> Does this mean we can't praise our children enthusiastically when they do something great? Should we try and restrain our admiration for their successes? Not at all. It just means that we should keep away from certain *kinds* [italics in original] of praise—praise that judges their intelligence or talent. Or praise that implies we're proud of them for their intelligence or talent rather than the work they've put in. We can

> praise them as much as we want for the growth-oriented process—what they accomplished through practice, study, perseverance, and good strategies. And we can ask them about their work in a way that admires and appreciates their effort and choices.

Dweck wisely adds that this advice applies not only to how we talk to our children about *themselves*; we should also avoid global judgments in how we talk about *others*.[23]

Here is an example of Dweck's advice in action. Journalist Po Bronson describes his effort to take Dweck's lessons to heart and to put them into practice with his kindergarten son, Luke.

> I tried to use the specific-type praise that Dweck recommends. I praised Luke, but I attempted to praise his "process." . . . Every night he has math homework and has to read a phonics book aloud. Each takes about five minutes if he concentrates, but he's easily distracted. So I praised him for concentrating without asking to take a break. After soccer games, I praised him for looking to pass, rather than just saying, "You played great." And if he worked hard to get the ball, I praised the effort he applied. Just as the research promised . . . it was remarkable how noticeably effective this new form of praise was.[24]

This is a wonderful example, from a thoughtful and devoted father. Note especially that, with his new approach, Bronson pays more attention to what Luke is doing—his effort as well as his frustrations along the way. And Luke gets *more*, not less, praise.

Praise Junkies?

Parenting advisor Alfie Kohn, in several books and articles, also presents a critique of praise. Kohn believes that frequent praise may create in children a hunger for external approval and a long-term sense of insecurity. He warns that our children may become, in this way, "praise junkies." Kohn's books include much thoughtful and wise advice. On this issue, however, I believe that his recommendations are wrong.

A child's need for praise and approval, for recognition and appreciation from admired adults, is not, as Kohn believes, an "extrinsic" reward. Candy, tokens, and money are extrinsic rewards. Praise—or a smile, or a gleam in our eye—is different. It is a deeply *intrinsic* human *need*, as important as any other. For this reason, when we praise our children, we do not create an addiction to praise. In fact, the opposite is true. Children are more likely to become praise junkies in the *absence* of our praise and approval.

When children feel proud, when they have been successful at any task, they instinctively look to others to share this feeling. Kids need this acknowledgment. Without sufficient praise, a child will suffer symptoms—especially discouragement and lack of enthusiasm—or he will seek this nutrient elsewhere, or he will become angry and demand praise, even if it has not been wholly earned. I therefore believe that we should offer children generous praise for all of their efforts, including their good behavior. Over time, they will come to learn that praise is earned—by hard work and good deeds.[25]

Anxiety

Children differ in their sensitivity to anxiety and fear. This dimension of children's temperament has been reliably established and is apparent very early in life. A young child's sensitivity to anxiety is a biological risk factor for the development of anxiety disorders in later childhood and adolescence.[26] It is also important for parents to know that some anxiety disorders in children (especially obsessive-compulsive disorder) are now recognized as essentially neurological disorders and require special treatment techniques.

Lorenz's Raven

Anxiety (like interest, and pride or shame) is almost continually present in our lives. At the very least, anxiety is a daily experience in the lives of our children, as they anticipate their interactions with parents, teachers, and peers. Emotion researcher Carroll Izard recalls Conrad Lorenz's example of the relationship between interest and anxiety. Lorenz watched a raven, perched on a high limb of a tall tree, cautiously approach an object on the ground. The raven first flew toward the object of his interest; he would then retreat to the safety of successively lower branches.[27]

Anxiety is a daily experience in the lives of our children.

Children, like Lorenz's raven, are interested, but also anxious, in their anticipation of any novel situation, for example, their first day of school or summer camp. They are anxious in anticipation of criticism and punishment; about separation, loss, and pain (and about their first encounter with a child therapist). They are especially anxious about experiences that may evoke feelings of shame (for example, social rejection, academic failure, or an evaluation or performance of any kind).

As attentive parents, we recognize this emotional state and, in many different ways—but especially with our presence and encouragement—we try to keep our children's anxiety within a tolerable range, so they can explore, then safely retreat, then explore again. In this way, children learn to approach new situations with greater interest and less fear.

Many well-intentioned parents attempt to help children cope with anxiety by telling their child that she should *not* be anxious. This is not possible, however, and therefore rarely helpful. Instead, children learn to cope with anxiety more successfully when parents help them to *tolerate* being anxious. It is better to help a child *be* anxious—to acknowledge her anxiety, to anticipate the situations that may make her afraid, and then to develop a problem-solving plan.

We should also let our children know that we are all anxious sometimes. We can then talk with them about our own experiences in similar situations and about how we coped.[28]

Mr. and Mrs. W consulted me about their 10-year-old son, Edward, who had seemed moody over the past few weeks and was having difficulty falling asleep. Edward's parents suspected that these problems might be caused by his anxiety about going away the next month for the first time, to summer camp.

I asked Edward how he felt about going to camp. He told me, "I *was* nervous, but my parents told me not to be nervous, that everything will be fine. They remind me of all the fun things I will be doing." I gently disagreed. "I think all kids are nervous the first time they go away to camp. They're also excited. It's a little bit of both. You haven't met the other kids yet, or your counselor, and that first moment, when you get on the bus, kids can feel pretty nervous—and also a little sad. There can be some other bad moments, too, especially at night, when you're not involved in an activity. Let's think about some things you can do, if you do feel bad, to make those bad moments a little better."

It goes without saying that, as parents, we are anxious about our children. We worry about their health and safety, their happiness, and their preparation for life. We worry about their future success, about what kind of children they are now, and about what kind of adults they will become. Parents who do not worry about their children are either preternaturally sanguine or (more likely) disengaged.

Anger

As parents, we pay perhaps more attention to our children's expressions of anger than to any other emotion. Although this is unfortunate, the reasons for our concern are understandable. We know the obvious destructive potential of anger, and the appropriate expression of anger is a primary concern of parents in all cultures. All children need to learn to modulate and channel their feelings of anger and to diminish the urgency and inflexibility of their angry reactions.

Anger has an obvious adaptive function. The purpose of anger is to defend ourselves—and those we love. In childhood and in adult life, anger is evoked by frustration, by feeling wronged, and by physical or emotional pain. We become angry when we are injured or held back, and at any potential harm to people or things we love and value.

What makes children most angry—and what keeps them angry—is a feeling of grievance, of unfairness. As I will discuss in a later chapter, child therapists have learned an important lesson of communicating with children: If a child is defiant, sullen, or uncommunicative, ask her about what is unfair in her life. She will almost always open up.

Research on anger in childhood leads to several conclusions that are important—and not surprising: Children who are able to regulate their expressions of anger are better liked by their peers as early as preschool; and a child's *inability* to regulate expressions of anger is a risk factor for emotional problems at all ages. When parents are often angry with their children, children show more emotional distress, more avoidant styles of interaction, poorer understanding of emotion, and less helping behavior toward their parents and peers.[29]

Parents need to prevent the buildup of anger in the minds of their children. A child who remains angry may begin to hold onto grievances, to inwardly build a case against offending others, and to develop a stubborn sense of unfairness and injustice. Chronic frustration, anger, and emotional pain lead all of us to harbor darker thoughts about others—and about ourselves. Like prolonged feelings of shame, prolonged anger is therefore profoundly harmful to children.[30]

If your child is defiant, sullen, or uncommunicative, ask her about what is unfair in her life. She will almost always open up.

Successful programs have been developed to help children learn improved anger management. Children are taught to reevaluate the events that evoke their anger and to think of alternative, less destructive methods of expressing angry thoughts and feelings. These programs have been refined and tested, and they are helpful to many children, teachers, and parents.[31]

But we can do more.

In my opinion, we are even more helpful if we define our task more broadly—when we identify the sources of our children's frustration and anger, and begin to repair feelings of resentment and grievance. We then not only help children "manage" their anger. They are less angry in the first place.

For all of us, being heard is the best form of anger management.

Sadness

Sadness is our instinctive response to loss, aloneness, and disappointment. We feel sadness especially at the loss of someone (or something) we deeply value, and at the loss of sources of affirmation and support—the loss of those who have helped us thrive.

Like all emotions, sadness has an essential biological function—children cry for a reason. The probable origin and purpose of expressions of sadness, in all mammals, is to elicit social support (especially in the form of physical touch) when children have been separated from their parents.[32]

In modern human life, however, sadness has come to serve a more general purpose: We learn from our sadness to appreciate, protect, and preserve what we value. Perhaps for this reason, in some cultures and historical eras (including, to some extent, our own) the experience of sadness has been regarded as a virtue, associated with maturity and wisdom. (As, for example, in Coleridge's famous poem "The Rime of the Ancient Mariner": "A sadder and a wiser man/he woke the morrow morn.")

Sadness and disappointment are also common, perhaps daily, events in the life of a child. Our children experience sadness in reaction to ordinary disappointments as well as profound sadness in response to extraordinary, traumatic events, for example, separation, divorce, or death. At these times, empathic parents offer solace and consolation to their children. We help our children learn that this sadness, however painful, will not last forever.

In this way, children learn to *tolerate* sadness and disappointment, an essential component of emotional health. When we help our children with their feelings of sadness, when we help them cope with disappointment and loss, we are not only helping them solve problems. We are helping them find meaning in life.

A child's effort to cope with loss and to preserve what she has loved is beautifully illustrated in two of my favorite books for children. *Geraldine's Blanket*, by Holly Keller, describes a young child's attachment to a security blanket. "Geraldine," the book begins, "had a pink blanket. Aunt Bessie sent it when Geraldine was a little baby. Geraldine took it everywhere with her." The blanket becomes worn and frayed, but Geraldine rebuffs all her parents' efforts to convince her to give up her blanket. Geraldine's parents then try a different approach. A new present arrives from Aunt Bessie—a wonderful doll named Rosa. Geraldine loves the new doll, but she still will not give up her blanket. Then Geraldine has an idea. She takes the now tattered blanket and makes it into a coat for Rosa. She says, "Now Rosa has the blanket and I have Rosa."[33]

In *My Grandmother's Cookie Jar*, by Montzalee Miller, a young Native American girl listens to the stories her grandmother lovingly tells her every night about "her Indian people of long ago," as they eat cookies together from a special jar. When the grandmother dies, the girl's grandfather consoles her. He brings her the empty cookie jar and gently explains, "The jar is full of Grandma's love and Indian spirit. When you are grown and have children of your own you will put cookies in the jar. The cookies will be dusted with Grandma's love. If you tell one of grandma's stories with each of the cookies, then her spirit and the spirit of those who went before her will live on." The young girl resolves, "I will keep the spirits alive. I will tell grandmother's stories."[34]

Most of us can probably recall moments of sadness or loneliness in our own lives, followed, when we are fortunate—as in

Miller's moving story—by a resolve to make this sadness meaningful by creating a more meaningful life. Feelings of sadness and loneliness are, perhaps, a universal accompaniment to the process of separation and individuation that normally occurs in adolescence and early adulthood. How we resolve these crises—and our sadness—comes to define, in large part, our character and guiding values.

In this chapter, I have tried to offer some new perspectives on several important emotions. Even in childhood, of course, our emotions are rarely simple; more often (as with Edward) they are mixed and complex. In the following chapters, I will show how parents' responsiveness to their children's emotions strengthens children's resilience and character. When we understand our children's feelings, we not only help them *feel* better, we help them *do* better—in all aspects of their lives.

Chapter 2

What Matters Most

Understanding and Support

Parents often ask, "Why does he continue to act this way—to tease or hit his sister, to refuse to do his homework or clean up his room, to lie when we know that he is lying and he knows that he will be punished?" Many parents (and some child therapists) assume that, in these situations, they have not been consistent enough in setting limits or imposing consequences for their child's bad behavior.

But the correct answer is almost always, "He behaves this way because he is caught up in the emotion of the moment." As we all are, at times.

Among child psychologists, a consensus has emerged. A child's increasing ability to "regulate" her emotions—to control and channel her expression of emotions, to express her feelings in constructive rather than hurtful ways—is now recognized as a critical factor in children's psychological health. Improved emotion regulation leads to benefits in all areas of a child's adjustment to life—increased attention to tasks, less disruptive behavior, better ability to resolve conflicts with peers, and lower levels of psychological and physical stress.[1]

Emotion is also our essential language in talking with children. It is through parents' recognition and responsiveness to their child's emotions that children feel known and understood. Neuroscientists Jaak Panksepp and Jeffrey Burgdorf write that emotions are "the currency of the mind/brain economy."[2]

When we talk with our children, we need to use this currency. When we talk with children about their emotions, we are always talking about what is *important* to them, what they care about and what *matters* to them—their needs and concerns, their "projects" and their goals.[3]

Good Feelings Versus Good People

In recent years, however, some cultural critics and parent advisors have argued that we now pay too *much* attention to our children's feelings. The critics believe that we have gone too far—that we have become too concerned with our children's *feelings* and not concerned enough with their *competence* and moral actions; that we are tuned in to their *desires* but not their *obligations*; that we focus too much attention on helping our children "feel good" and not enough on helping them become "good people."[4]

In this view, we have tried so hard to make our children happy that we've made them unhappy. We are so concerned that they not feel any disappointment ("Will he be too upset?") and with their self-esteem that we no longer provide them with the experience of mastering challenges—experiences of mastery that lead to the strengthening of character and real, earned, self-esteem. We offer them too many choices, fail to make appropriate demands, and allow them too often to say no.

Emotion is our essential language in talking with children.

The eminent developmental psychologist William Damon, for example, warns that "child-centered beliefs have encouraged exaggerated concerns about children's momentary feelings."[5] Damon (and many others) argues that, in place of discipline and guidance, contemporary parenting practices have fostered a culture of indulgence that is harmful to our society—and to our children.

Many contemporary parents, Damon observes, have become "afraid of their children." We are afraid of their tantrums and therefore give in to their selfish and unreasonable demands. Our children, in this view, come to learn that only *their* feelings and their achievements, not service or responsibility to others, matter.[6] As a result, in Damon's opinion, too many of our children have become demoralized—dispirited and lacking a sense of moral purpose. Parents now "expect less and receive less in return."[7]

These criticisms find frequent support in the daily press. We hear of "helicopter" parents who constantly hover over their children; or, more recently, of "curling" parents, named for the Winter Olympic sport of curling. Curling parents, it is said, like the Olympic athletes, try to smooth the path ahead of their children. Instead of teaching their children to overcome obstacles through their own effort and hard work, curling parents try to remove even the smallest friction or bad feeling from their child's path through life.[8]

Although I do not fully agree with this critique, it does have some merit. It is not difficult, in our everyday lives, to find appalling examples of parental indulgence. Damon, for example, observes parents who do not prevent, or even admonish, children who blatantly violate the rights of others—parents who watch idly as a boy grabs a bicycle from his younger brother or as a child takes a pen from a cashier in a store.[9]

But there are also problems with these kinds of claims.

I agree that our children are demoralized, and I wholeheartedly endorse what Damon considers the fundamental goals of child rearing—the development of "competence and character" in our children. I also share with Damon and others a concern about the epidemic of narcissism and "unbridled individualism" in our contemporary culture.[10] The symptoms of our children's demoralization—depression, defiant and self-destructive behavior emerging more frequently and earlier in life—are real and alarming.[11] And our narcissism is everywhere.

The *causes* of their demoralization, however, are less certain, and many of the remedies prescribed may be off the mark. We need to ask, have we indulged them—or failed to inspire them?

In my clinical experience, the most frequent cause of demoralization in children is not indulgence and certainly not an exaggerated concern with their momentary feelings. Far more often, we pay too *little* attention to our children's feelings—their worries, their disappointments, and their frustrations. So much of our conflict and our disconnection from our children, so much of their discouragement and withdrawal, comes not from a failure of discipline but from our failure to listen to their concerns. In my experience, greater understanding—more often than greater expectations—is the solution to the problem of a child's demoralization.

In my practice, I have met some very self-centered children and some curling parents. I have certainly encountered many instances of indulgent parenting, and I have met parents who, whether from exhaustion or from a sense of their child's "specialness," too readily give in to their child's demands.[12] Far more often, however, I meet concerned and caring parents who have become (again, despite their best intentions) angry and critical. And their children, in turn, have become argumentative and stubborn, or secretive and withdrawn. Yes, we may often be indulgent—buying them too much and giving in to unreasonable demands—but more often we are "at them"—nagging and yelling, telling them what they should be doing and what they are doing wrong.

These families are locked in vicious cycles of criticism and defiance that undermine children's initiative, confidence, and sense of responsibility. As these cycles escalate, parents feel increasingly justified in their criticism and disapproval, and kids, for their part, feel increasingly justified in their resentment and defiance. Parents tell me, "He never listens." The child tells me, "All I hear is criticism" or "They are always yelling at me."

Empathy

And, in this debate, empathy and understanding, which remain the essence of good parenting, have gotten a bad name—and a bum rap. Many parent advisors who believe that our children need more consistent limits are skeptical of empathy. In this view, empathy comes too close to indulgence—an oversolicitous concern with the child's feelings, at the expense of the feelings and rights of others.[13]

These fears, however, are for the most part unfounded.

Empathy is not indulgence. A parent's effort to understand her child's feelings and appreciate her concerns is not permissive and it is not laissez-faire. Listening with empathy helps children bounce back. In our concern with standards and discipline, we should not lose sight of a simple truth: Our children will be more willing to listen to us when we have first listened to them.

Our children will be more willing to listen to us when we have first listened to them.

When we are able to convey empathic understanding to our children, when children feel that their concerns—and their grievances—have been heard, they will make *fewer, not more* demands. They will be *better* behaved and more caring toward others. And we will have an easier time when it is time to say no.

Child-Centered Versus Parent-Centered Parenting

This debate, however, is generations, even centuries, old and unlikely to go away. In her book *Raising America*, a history of expert advice offered to parents over the course of the 20th century, Ann Hulbert finds in every generation two competing traditions of child rearing. She refers to these as "child-centered" and "parent-centered" parenting philosophies.

Advocates of a parent-centered philosophy believe, especially, in the importance of a child's obedience to adult authority. In this view, good relationships (and good feelings) follow from good behavior. Advocates of a child-centered philosophy believe otherwise—that good behavior follows from good feelings. Not surprisingly, these philosophies are based less on scientific evidence and far more on the differing personalities and values of their proponents. They represent different views of the nature of childhood, of what children need to thrive and succeed, and what kind of person our society needs to maintain our values and our place in the world.[14]

In real life, as Hulbert demonstrates, these are often false choices. Discipline without empathy may produce some short-term obedience but at great risk of long-term defiance that is ultimately destructive of initiative and responsibility. And empathy without moral guidance *is* indulgent and may foster unrealistic expectations that also undermine a child's initiative and resilience.

The solution to this debate is therefore simple in theory, if often difficult in everyday life. Feelings matter. Behavior also matters. Our children need to know that their feelings are important but so are the needs and feelings of others. We need to encourage their self-expression and *also* teach them self-restraint.

There will always be some tension between our empathic concerns (our desire to comfort our children, to protect them from disappointment, to help them feel better *now*) and our socializing concerns (our desire, for example, to teach them more mature ways of managing distress, to work harder, to learn the skills they will need to do well in life). There will always be some tension between letting them have fun (and giving in a little more than we should) and insisting on rules and limits. Most of us, as parents, struggle to find the right balance between these competing concerns.[15]

What Matters Most

To the extent that sides must be chosen, I side with the child-centered approach, for several reasons. In the parent-centered model, if we want to change our children's feelings, we should help them change their behavior. We should challenge them to meet higher expectations, to act responsibly, to work hard, and to do good deeds. The goals are laudable, but the methods are often questionable.

Parent-centered advisors believe that children will behave well when they know what is expected of them and when they come to understand the consequences of their actions. Clinical experience has taught me, however, that often this is not true. Angry and discouraged children do not behave well, regardless of the consequences of their behavior.

And we now know that frequent references to rules and consequences, even strict enforcement of rules and consequences, is simply not the best way to foster good behavior in young children.[16] If we want our children to be well behaved, we should play (and work) with them often, offer encouragement and support for their interests and projects, use reasoning and discussion in the solution of problems,[17] repair moments of anger and criticism, and let them know that we are proud of them, especially for the good things they do for others.

Then, we can set limits. We can let them know when their demands or their behavior is "over the line" (and, when necessary, institute a simple system of earning rewards and privileges for cooperation with basic tasks). But no system of rewards and punishments, even rewards for generous behavior, can produce a generous spirit.

Decades of child development research support the conclusion that our responsiveness, as parents, to our children's emotions is good for our children. Children who are able to regulate their emotions, children who are confident that their feelings and concerns will be heard, will behave well (most of the time). They will more easily make and keep friends; they will show more empathy and caring; and they will work harder and achieve more in school.[18]

No system of rewards and punishments, even rewards for generous behavior, can produce a generous spirit.

Over time, I have come to a personal philosophy about the nature of childhood and some simple conclusions about being a parent, conclusions that are often obscured in contemporary parenting debates. I believe that what matters most in our children's emotional development—and to their success in life—is not how strict or how permissive we are, but our children's inner certainty of our interest, encouragement, and support. Our children look up to us and they want to do well. What matters most is that we share their joys and offer solace for their sadness and disappointments. What matters most is our willingness to repair the conflicts that will inevitably occur in our relationships with our children, our willingness to help them overcome their mistakes, and to let them know that we are proud of them—for their effort and their accomplishments. In these ways, we strengthen our children's inner resources. We help them bounce back from setbacks of all kinds, and we remain a source of ideals and moral guidance—ideals that provide a sense of purpose and meaning in their lives.[19]

Chapter 3

Optimism and Resilience Versus Demoralization and Defiance

All children, even the most fortunate, suffer emotional injuries. At home, in school, and on the playground, all children experience disappointment, frustration, and failure; criticism and disapproval; and exclusion by peers. All children experience moments when they feel discouraged and alone, even unloved.

A child is told by her classmates, "We do not want you to play with us." Or he is playing baseball and, as we all do, he strikes out. Or she may watch as other children read fluently aloud to their teacher, while she reads haltingly and feels silently ashamed. An adult relative of mine struggled with reading as a child. She recalls being asked to read aloud in her fourth-grade Hebrew school class. She remembers her embarrassment and humiliation, and the critical tone of her teacher's words. She never went to Hebrew school again.

For every child, these are injuries. Each of these common experiences makes children feel ashamed and often angry. Every injury also evokes in children some self-protective behavior—some form of protest, retaliation, or withdrawal, and some hardening of her protective shell.

In health, children are able to bounce back.

Too often, however, children do not quickly bounce back. Painful feelings linger, longer than they should. Over time, demoralization and defiant attitudes take hold and family interactions increasingly take the form of vicious cycles. Criticism and punishment lead to anger and defiance, or secretiveness and withdrawal; and then to more criticism; and then more defiance and more withdrawal.

In this chapter I will describe these healthy and unhealthy events in a child's life, and I will begin a discussion of how we can put our children on the right path—a path toward resilience and emotional health.

Positive Expectations

Psychological health, in childhood and throughout life, depends on our ability to hold onto positive emotions and, especially, positive *expectations*.[1] Long-term studies of disadvantaged children consistently lead to this conclusion: Children who succeed despite adversity are those who are able to maintain positive expectations for their futures. And these children have the support of someone they admire and who believes in them.[2]

Positive expectations keep kids on the right track. Positive expectations for their futures help children and adolescents make good decisions and work hard in the present. Children with positive expectations will also more readily accept their parents' discipline, because they will understand the need for it.

Positive expectations for their futures help children and adolescents make good decisions—and work hard—in the present.

Children who do well in life—in school, in nonacademic pursuits, and with their peers—are able to bounce back from disappointment and defeat, to learn from their failures and their mistakes, to restore some good feeling about themselves (and about others), and to sustain effort toward goals that are important to them. This essential aspect of emotional maturity has many names. We call this emotional resilience, optimism, or "psychological immunity."[3]

Repair

Emotional injuries are, in many respects, analogous to physical injuries, and emotional health is in many ways analogous to physical health. Just as our cells must repair physical injuries, emotional injuries also must be healed. Without this healing, the injurious process will spread. When we suffer a physical injury, we instinctively withdraw in pain, and the site of the injury becomes inflamed. It is the same with emotional injuries. Children protest and withdraw, and until their injuries are healed, they become less inclined to seek challenges and take risks.

Our task as parents is to recognize these common injuries and to help our children bounce back, to provide some healing of their discouragement and anger. Often, a simple acknowledgment of a child's disappointment or frustration is all that is necessary.

Children derive from these experiences—of emotional injury, followed by repair—essential aspects of healthy personality development. They learn that their distress is temporary (and therefore bearable) and that through their own actions, or with the help of supportive adults, they can make things better. They learn that that this bad feeling will not last forever, that they will do better in the future, and that there are other good things to look forward to—that there will be, as Julia said, a "next time."

In healthy development, this is how children learn to cope with frustration and disappointment. When emotional injuries are repaired, children learn that disappointments, in themselves and in others, are part of life and that feelings of anger and unfairness do not last forever. The result, over time, is optimism and resilience.

A Fulcrum Shift

But there is more. When children are able to bounce back from frustration and disappointment, maturing processes take place. Children with positive expectations are open to learning—and to caring. Resilient children are more successful in their peer relationships, better able to take into account the needs of others, more willing to compromise, and more open to the socializing efforts of their parents and teachers.

In talking with children, when we are able to help them bounce back, we set in motion a fulcrum shift in a child's emotional development—a shift that leads the child *away* from urgent and insistent demands and *toward* initiative, problem solving, and acceptance of personal responsibility.

When emotional injuries are repaired, children become less absorbed in defiant thoughts and argument, less urgent in their expressions of distress, and less insistent in their demands. We will also have been able, at least in that moment, to stop the spread of pessimistic attitudes and beliefs (for example, when children feel that "No one *ever* listens to me"; "I am *always* disappointed"; or "I *always* stink"). Moments of repair may also lead to a reduction in the level of stress hormones and other stress-related processes that, when prolonged, are damaging to children's physical and emotional health.[4]

Unhealthy Emotional Development: Demoralization, Defiance, and Vicious Cycles

Paul was an intelligent and engaging 10-year-old boy with a wide range of interests. Paul's parents described him, from a very early age, as mischievous and impulsive but also sensitive and sad, given to sullen, dark moods. For long periods of time, Paul seemed generally happy, and in one-on-one interactions with either of his parents, he was enthusiastic, playful, and cooperative. But Paul also wanted a lot; he was often relentless in his demands and he could become intensely angry. Although he was a good student, when he became frustrated Paul would tear up his homework, and he frequently told his parents that he "hates school." Recently, Mr. and Mrs. A described a downward spiral in Paul's mood and behavior. Paul was often angry; he complained that the punishments he received were unfair, and at times he expressed the feeling that he was "bad."

I had met Paul a few years earlier, when Mr. and Mrs. A consulted me about similar concerns, and I worked with Paul and his parents for a brief period of therapy. Paul played with enthusiasm and he spoke with unusual openness. During these initial meetings, Mr. A mentioned that Paul often woke up early, and he enjoyed taking a walk with his father to the corner store to buy the morning newspaper. I encouraged Mr. A to make these early morning walks a daily routine, and both Paul and his father readily agreed. Paul's mood and behavior soon improved. Although he was still mischievous and impulsive, Paul's parents reported that he seemed more accepting of disappointments and less insistent in his demands.

Mr. and Mrs. A called for occasional consultations, when Paul's impulsive or defiant behavior had again caused concern. At these times, Paul was usually happy to talk, at least for a few sessions. On one occasion, Paul described recent interactions he had had with his mother. In his own words, he identified a very common unhealthy family process:

> I don't like the rules . . . . so I'll say something . . . . and she thinks I'm being fresh . . . and she'll take something away . . . like my screen time . . . . and that makes me mad . . . and then *it stays with me*. . . . and she thinks I'm always mad . . . .

it's a big cycle . . . .when I'm with my friends, it all dissolves away.

This last statement was hardly reassuring.

Several months later, I was again talking with Paul. I reminded him of our earlier discussion and how he had described to me the cycle of bad feelings that happens so often in his family—and in many other families. He now added, "You forgot the part where the kid apologizes, but the mom is still angry." With this comment, Paul identified yet another critical aspect of these unhealthy interactions: the failure of a child's efforts at repair.

Paul was demoralized and angry. Although he was interested and capable in many things—in music, in creative writing, in sports, and in his knowledge of history—to his parents' great dismay, he did not pursue any of these interests with enthusiasm or commitment. In his academic work, especially, but in everything he did, Paul rushed through, and he gave up quickly when he encountered the slightest frustration.

There was good reason to be concerned about his future.

Mrs. A loved her children, but she clashed with Paul. His moodiness and his demands, and his meanness toward his siblings, were understandably difficult for her. In her frustration, she would often react with harsh statements (for example, "What is wrong with you?") and with frequent punishments—punishments that would have been reasonable if they had been brief but went on far too long. (Mr. and Mrs. A held the common, although incorrect, theory that punishments, to be effective, must be severe; otherwise, they believed, Paul wouldn't care). Mrs. A asked, "Why is he like this?" This is always a difficult question to answer. For most unhappy children, there are many complex, intertwined reasons that are impossible to separate.

Over time, Paul began to doubt that his mother loved him and whether he loved her. Both Paul and his mother, in their anger, said hurtful things to each other—statements that, although they both wanted to make things better, were difficult to repair.

Paul admired his father and he wanted his father to be proud of him. But these feelings had become buried, and Paul would often say that he didn't care. He didn't care about punishments and he didn't care about school. He wasn't one of the smart kids anyway.

But he did care.

In unhealthy emotional development, painful feelings—feelings of discouragement and resentment, moments of failure, criticism, or social rejection—linger in the mind of the child. As Paul said, "It stays with me."

A child's thoughts and imagination are then likely to take a defiant turn, a turn toward demoralization or rebellion, and away from us. Emotional injuries that are not repaired lead to prolonged feelings of discouragement or aloneness, or resentment and grievance. Over time, all aspects of a child's emotional life are increasingly drawn into the orbit of painful feelings. Discouragement, aloneness, and resentment are the enemies of resilience, and harmful to a child's initiative and sense of responsibility.

> **Discouragement, aloneness, and resentment are the enemies of resilience.**

For Paul and his parents, the path to better family relationships was not an easy one. There were more angry moments, and these moments were not always quickly repaired. Over time, however, Mr. and Mrs. A became better able to understand Paul's hurt feelings, and Paul became less stuck in his angry moods. Medicine for attention-deficit/hyperactivity disorder (ADHD) (a difficult decision for Mr. and Mrs. A) helped Paul put more consistent effort into his schoolwork. Paul is now on a better path. He pursues his interests with greater enthusiasm and commitment, and he is more understanding of his parents' values and concerns.

Discouragement: Tool of the Devil

For all of us, some brief feeling of discouragement (and some temporary experience of shame) follows every academic failure, every competitive defeat, every social rejection, and every failure to elicit expressions of pride and approval from admired others. In health, we recover from these moments. We find a way to restore our sense of hopefulness and possibility. Troubled children do not quickly recover. They remain, longer than they should, demoralized and angry.[5]

A child may, at times, express her demoralization openly. She may think (and sometimes say), "I will never be popular" or "I will never be a good student" or "I will never be able to get rid of this bad feeling."

Often, of course, children deny these feelings. Their discouragement is hidden, masked by stubbornness and blaming of others. We see their discouragement, instead, in their pessimism and in their lack of initiative and long-term goals.

Children who are demoralized are also more envious (openly or privately) of other children—their siblings or their peers. Many demoralized children believe (in any effort to find the cause of their bad feelings) that their parents and teachers make unreasonable demands. Students with learning disabilities always experience some degree of demoralization. An essential aspect of our task as parents (and mine as a child therapist) is to mitigate, or cure, this demoralization—to restore and strengthen a child's feeling of hope.[6]

I recently found support for these ideas in an unexpected place. In the NFL Films documentary *Hard Knocks*, Mike Westhoff, special teams coach of the New York Jets, tells his players a story about the devil. In this tale, the devil, when asked what is his most useful tool, answers, "Discouragement. Because discouragement makes all my other tools more effective." Coach Westhoff then exhorts his players not to give in to discouragement, this tool of the devil.

Defiance

Defiance is another pathway of unhealthy emotional development. Like demoralization, a child's defiance may take many forms. Children often express their defiance as stubbornness or argument, or as sarcasm and disrespect. A child's defiance may be expressed openly (for example, in oppositional behavior, in not speaking, or in lying) or covertly, in his attitudes and imagination.

A child who is publicly ridiculed by his teacher (or privately ridiculed by a parent) may not *say* "F... you" to his parent or teacher. But he will *think* "F... you." This attitude will then find some expression in his imagination or behavior, perhaps as disparagement or contempt.[7]

Ominously, persistent defiant attitudes result in an inner destruction of our authority—and our influence—as parents. A child begins to feel, "I don't care what they think." Our children continue to need us, however, as sources of guidance and support. They are vulnerable, and often headed for trouble, when they no longer care what we think.[8]

Vicious Cycles

Vicious cycles of criticism and defiance are the most common form of unhealthy family interactions. These cycles often begin when a child's impulsive or immature behavior elicits critical reactions from his parents, his teachers, or his peers. He may overhear other children saying, "Don't play with Jeremy, he's annoying." Or we are angry and he tells us, "I didn't do anything wrong."

These critical responses reinforce a child's sense of injury. He now feels badly about himself and angry at others. He is more likely to withdraw from peer interactions, to persist in his immature behavior, or to respond, either in the present or at some later time, with more defiance. He may begin to act "weird" or provocative with his peers or to think of himself as one of the "bad" kids; and he may retaliate—with actions that perpetuate a cycle of anger and alienation.

Over time, defiant interactions escalate. Arguments become louder, angrier, and more stubborn, and less provocation is needed to evoke a defiant response. A child's (or parent's) anger may now be triggered by a seemingly neutral or innocuous comment or question, or by a roll of the eyes.

In my experience, every child—no matter how angry or discouraged, secretive or seemingly unmotivated—at the same time wants her parents' approval and wants to do well.

In my clinical experience, some degree of *both* demoralization and defiance are usually present in the emotional lives of troubled children. These feelings are conveyed in the complaints I so often hear from unhappy children, when children tell me, for example, "I hate school," "I hate my teachers," or "I hate my life."

But every child, no matter how angry and discouraged, no matter how defiant, secretive, or unmotivated she may seem to be, at the same time wants her parents' approval, wants to do well, and wants to be accepted by her peers. The solution to the emotional and behavior problems of childhood begins with this fact.

What Can We Do?

As parents, how can we promote emotional resilience in our children? How can we help our children bounce back and maintain positive expectations for their futures?

To begin, we *listen*.

We offer encouragement and support for our children's projects and appreciation of their concerns. When they are excited, share their excitement. When they are anxious, frustrated, or disappointed, offer empathy, solace, and understanding. Let them know that you know how they feel—because you have also had these feelings. Talk with them about your own disappointments and frustrations, and about how you coped with them.

Many years ago, at the beginning my clinical practice, I was working with Alan, a troubled 13-year-old boy, who often spent much of his sessions in silence. One day, Alan told me about being bullied at school. I chose to tell Alan, honestly, that I had also been bullied at his age. The following week, Alan entered my office and immediately asked, "You know that story you told me last week, about being picked on, tell me again."

Patient listening has gone out of style in our current preoccupation with "strategies" and finding quick solutions to a child's problematic behavior. But, at the end of the day, there is no more important parenting skill than this—and nothing that we do as parents that is more important to our children's success in life.

Your constant presence in the life of your child as a source of emotional support is, I believe, your most essential task as a parent, and continues throughout her life. Your child's inner expectation of your recognition and approval—that you are proud of her and believe she is capable of doing good things—sustains her during inevitable moments of anxiety, discouragement, and failure.[9]

We all need this support, at every stage of life. So often, however, concerned and caring parents erode their support of their children with frequent admonishments and criticism. As we try and get our children to *improve*, to do better, we undermine our support of them and unwittingly create defiance and resentment.

Our goal as parents is not to eliminate our children's frustrations and disappointments but to help them bounce back. We help them put their disappointments in perspective and repair damage to their positive expectations. When we are successful, we will observe this healthy development in more successful peer relationships, in less urgent and inflexible demands, and in less frequent avoidance and withdrawal—overall, a more confident, joyful, and responsible participation in life.

Chapter 4

Positiveness

All parents delight in the emergence of their young child's developing skills. We are charmed by young children, by their unabashed expressions of exuberance and glee, their excitement about what they are now, for the first time, able to do. And we take pride in our children's achievements, large and small. As we should.

Most parents would agree that children are likely to thrive in a family atmosphere of positiveness[1]—when we are able to be supportive and encouraging, and nurture in our children positive expectations for their futures. In the daily life of many families, however, positiveness has been eroded. Too often, parents have been reduced to not much more than taxiing their children to and from their various activities or making sure that they have done their homework or cleaned their rooms.

In this chapter, I will explain why positiveness is essential to children's emotional health, and I will discuss ways that parents can restore positiveness in their relationships with their children.

Sharing Positive Feelings

Two decades ago, child development expert Robert Emde called attention to the importance of positive emotions in the lives of young children. Emde began an influential essay with the observation that positive emotions, especially joy—so obvious to unbiased observers of new parents and their children—had been overlooked in most theories of child development. Joy was notably absent, for example, in Freud's theory.

Toward the end of the first year of life, children begin to look to others to share a positive feeling. A toddler will smile, for example, while he is exploring a room, and he looks toward his parent. Parents then instinctively respond to their child's smile with smiles of their own. Emde refers to this behavior as "positive affect sharing."[2]

Positive affect sharing occurs frequently in most families. It is part of our instinctive enjoyment of the wonders of child development. Unless other factors interfere (these could be fatigue, preoccupation, depression, or misguided ideology), positive affect sharing will be present in the interactions of almost all parents and young children. Teenage mothers, however—mothers whose children are at high risk for emotional and behavioral problems—rarely respond in this way with their children.[3]

Positive affect sharing is deeply rewarding to both children and parents. But it is not a "reward" in the narrow sense of the word. When we return a child's first smiles or reach out our arms to catch her as she takes her first steps,[4] we are not attempting to shape or reinforce our child's behavior. We have, however, strengthened something more important. We have strengthened her inner expectation of a joyful and encouraging response to her own instinctive expressions of enjoyment and pride.[5] Recall, also, that moments of mutual joy and delight between parents and infants may directly promote brain development in infancy.[6]

Sharing joyful feelings remains a need in all of us, throughout life. Without this, we can (perhaps) get by, but we will not get by well. We will struggle, more than many others do, with some degree of pessimism, resentment, and envy.

Lessons From Positive Psychology

The emerging field of positive psychology offers new insights into the benefits of positive emotions throughout our lives. Positive emotions have been shown to broaden our thinking; to speed our recovery from emotional distress; and to improve our health, our longevity, and the success of our marriages and partnerships. Positive emotions increase our productivity at work and our willingness to give to others.[7]

We spend far too much time correcting our children's mistakes, trying to help them improve, and not enough time recognizing their "signature strengths."

Psychologist Martin Seligman reviews many of these results in his important book, *Authentic Happiness*. Seligman also reports a personal insight, a lesson he learned from his then 5-year-old daughter. "Raising children," Seligman realized, was about "far more than just fixing what was wrong with them. It was about identifying and amplifying their strengths and virtues and helping them find the niche where they can live these positive traits to the fullest."

I agree. We spend far too much time correcting our children's mistakes, trying to help them improve, and not enough time recognizing and valuing what Seligman calls their "signature strengths." Seligman suggests that, for all of us, our satisfaction in life derives, more than anything else, from the combination of engaging our signature strengths in a way that also helps others.[8]

Staying Positive

A plan to improve our children's emotional health therefore begins with an effort to strengthen positiveness in family life. Increased positiveness is a first step toward strengthening our relationships with our children—and toward more cooperative behavior.

As parents, we can create positiveness in our relationships with our children in many ways: through enthusiastic interest and animated play; with expressions of appreciation; with an understanding of our children's "becoming" and the importance of a growth mindset; with personal sharings; and with our willingness to offer children generous praise—not for their intelligence or their talents, but for their effort and for the good things they do for others.

Interest and Play

My therapeutic work with children has taught me, over and over, a fundamental lesson: Children respond to our animated expressions of *interest* in their *interests* with evident pleasure. Children enjoy this interaction and they want more of it. Often, when I begin therapy with a child, after even a brief period of animated play, he may comment, "Mommy, this is fun. Can you sign me up for this?" or "Can I come here every day?"

Young children, particularly, but adolescents also, are almost always willing, and usually eager, to share their interests. Almost all children, except in moments of extreme sullenness or withdrawal, respond positively to any person's genuine interest in learning about their interests. In three decades of talking with children, I have met few, if any, children who did not want to share their interests with their parents—and few who were not deeply disappointed when their parents, for whatever reason, did not respond with enthusiasm. Children in therapy frequently tell me, "I tried to show this to my mom, but she wasn't interested." This leads, first, to sadness and disappointment and, later, to resentment and withdrawal.

When parents respond with animated, enthusiastic interest in their child's interests, most children soon begin to show more enthusiasm and emotional aliveness (and, often, less stubbornness). They are also likely to recover more quickly from moments of discouragement and frustration. These positive interactions seem to operate as a protective factor in children's emotional lives, to confer some degree of immunity against the effects of emotional distress.[9]

Parents need to frequently and actively share in their children's interests, on a daily basis, beyond being present at their performances and athletic events. I therefore ask parents, in every initial consultation, "What does your child like to do?" and "Is there some way that you can more frequently share in this interest with her?"[10]

Mr. and Mrs. S consulted me about their 8-year-old son, John. They expressed concern about John's frequent temper tantrums, his uncooperativeness, and his disregard of personal hygiene. John was a good student, but he often seemed unhappy. To his teachers, John's unhappiness was palpable. In school, John was aloof. He rarely spoke to other children, except for his one friend; he did not participate in any sports or games, or in academic projects that required either imagination or collaboration with other students; and on at least one occasion he had alarmed his teachers with vague references to "shooting" while standing apart from his classmates on the playing field.

When I first met John, he was standing, cowering, in the corner of my waiting room, while his two younger brothers played on the floor with blocks. Soon, however, John began to talk about his interest in the *Stars Wars* saga and the *Star Wars* computer games that occupied all of his free time. I asked John whether he played these games with his father. John looked puzzled. "No," he answered, "he has his *own* computer."

I recommended to Mr. S that he spend some time each evening playing with John, especially the *Star Wars* computer games John enjoyed and knew so much about. Mr. S readily agreed, and the effect of this simple suggestion was quite dramatic. John's mood brightened; he began to do his homework immediately after school, "so I can have time to play with my dad." There was still a long way to go in helping John after this initial progress, especially in helping him make friends. But he had taken a first step, and he was already a happier (and more cooperative) child.

Psychological Nutrition

When you follow your child's interest—her curiosity and excitement—you strengthen her confident expectation of your affirming responsiveness. You also nurture her intelligence and creativity, and her communication and problem-solving skills. Playing with your children promotes the enhancement and refinement of their social skills, as they learn to create increasingly complex interpersonal and emotional narratives. (I will continue this discussion of the importance of play in children's social and behavioral development in Chapter 6.)[11]

Many concerned and caring parents, however, whether for reasons of personality or life circumstance, find it difficult to play with their children. Some parents feel that they lack the time, or the interest, for play. But even small amounts—small doses—of enthusiastic interest and interactive play may be helpful to children.

If you are able to find opportunities for more frequent play and playfulness with your children, you will be rewarded—with increased pleasure in being a parent. And your children, sensing your pleasure, will more often and more eagerly seek out this engagement. You will have then set in motion a cycle of *positive* interactions, an antidote to the vicious cycles of criticism and defiance that are so common in the lives of modern families.

Interactive play is a first recommendation, or "prescription," for the healthy parenting of all children.

I think of positive affect sharing and responsive play as the psychological equivalent of good nutrition. Nutrition does not prevent all diseases or cure diseases once they have reached a certain stage. Still, good psychological nutrition is essential to emotional health and helps promote psychological immunity. And we know that these moments are important in the lives of our children—because children tell us about them. I therefore make interactive play a first recommendation, or "prescription," for the healthy parenting of all children.

Appreciation

The psychologist and philosopher William James once wrote to a student, "The deepest principle in human nature is the craving to be appreciated."

James' statement (thanking his student for a gift) may have been half in jest, and I don't know if James was entirely right in this belief. There are, of course, other principles and cravings in human nature. It is certainly true, however, that expressions of appreciation are invaluable in all relationships, including parent–child relationships.

Appreciation is a little bit like oxygen. We can survive with less than optimal oxygen, but we do not survive well. We suffer symptoms—some visible, others insidious. It is the same with appreciation. Without enough appreciation, we begin to suffer vague symptoms—especially diminished enthusiasm—although we may not know what is causing them. Without this psychological oxygen, our minds begin to divert resources and energy, resources that should be used to pursue interests and joy, into self-protective attitudes—defensiveness and demands. We become resentful and secretive.

Appreciation is the antidote for resentment.

We should express appreciation often to our children—for the little things they do, for their cooperation and helpfulness, and for their expressions of concern for others (especially their siblings). If we say "thank you" to them they will more often say "thank you" to us.

A Language of Becoming

Family therapist Ellen Wachtel has described another important way that we can remain positive with our children. Wachtel advises parents to cultivate, in talking with their children, a "language of becoming." A language of becoming is "a way of speaking to our children that enables them to see themselves as continually evolving and changing" and "developing emotional strengths." Wachtel explains that this way of speaking allows us to notice a child's "new actions" and focus on what is positive and hopeful, rather than problematic, in his behavior.

She offers this example: "When a child has had an explosive episode but eventually calms himself down and talks about the problem rationally, a parent has the choice of focusing either on the explosion or on how the youngster was able to calm himself down enough to have a rational discussion about the problem." Focusing on how he was able to calm himself supports his developing maturity.

Wachtel also reminds us of other affirming experiences, moments in our children's lives that may be of lasting importance:

> Most of us have had at one time or another the experience of being "discovered." Perhaps it was a visiting aunt, or a teacher, or a boyfriend who saw in us something that transformed—or at least greatly influenced—how we saw ourselves. Many people can remember a compliment, comment, or reflection on themselves that stuck with them for their entire lives. . . . These statements serve as emotional life preservers in stormy seas.[12]

Sharings

Young children are wide eyed in their curiosity about the lives of their parents. For many years, I have advised parents to talk with their children about experiences in their own lives, especially at times of sadness, anxiety, or disappointment. Personal sharings are helpful, for example, when children are anxious about their first day at school or summer camp, or an upcoming exam; or when they have suffered a painful rejection by a friend; or when they face difficulties in school; or when there has been a death in the family.

Telling personal stories to children, and in the presence of children, is an important child-rearing practice in many cultures. Often, these are cautionary tales, of dangers to avoid (or of virtues to be admired). Personal sharings also offer implicit hope to a discouraged child. In my experience, there is simply no better way, as a parent or as a therapist, to engage a young child's attention and provide emotional support than these humanizing personal disclosures.

I learned the value of telling personal stories when I was a young parent. Our daughter, Rachel, was not yet 3 years old when our son, Dan, was born. The baby slept in a bassinet in our bedroom for a few months until it was time for him to share a bedroom with his sister. Until now, Rachel had seemed pleased with her new role as a big sister, and she had expressed little jealousy of her baby brother. But this night, when going to bed, she told me, "I don't want my baby brother sleeping in my room."

Personal sharings offer implicit hope to a discouraged child.

This, I thought, would be any easy problem to solve, a piece of cake. I was, after all, a child psychologist, and this was Child Psych 101. I told Rachel that I could understand her feelings. We were able to give her less attention now than before the baby was born. And this room used to be *her* room; now, it was *the children's* room. Rachel quietly listened to my sympathetic explanations and, when I had finished, she replied, "Well, that's OK, but I still don't want my baby brother sleeping in my room."

Not knowing what else to do, I offered a personal story. "Let me tell you about when Daddy was a little boy and I slept in the same room with Uncle Bob and Uncle Steve." Rachel's eyes widened. To this point, she had listened with polite attention; now, she listened with rapt attention. I told her a (true) story about sharing a room with my brothers and she quickly fell asleep. Then, the following night and for several months thereafter, as I put her to bed, she asked, "Tell me a story about when you were a little boy."

There are many more ways that we can be positive with our children. Throughout this book, I will offer additional recommendations to strengthen positiveness in our family lives.

Positiveness, however, is not enough. I have met families where parents express frequent interest and positiveness, but kids are still often angry and defiant. These parents are understandably puzzled by their children's stubbornness and disrespect. I will now turn to these problems—why they happen and what we can do.

Chapter 5

Repair

The lives of children, of course, are not all about positive emotions. For every child (as for all of us) there is frustration and worry, envy and disappointment. All children will protest and misbehave, and refuse to do what we ask. In every family, there will be moments of anger and misunderstanding.

We now know that the repair of these moments is essential to our children's emotional health. Repair is essential to all of our relationships—our relationship with our children and the health of our marriages and partnerships. As parents, our willingness to repair conflict and heal painful emotions offers a second opportunity to strengthen our children's psychological immunity; along with positiveness, repair is another important pathway toward emotional health.

The Harmfulness of Criticism

If I were asked to identify the most common problem presented to me in three decades of therapeutic work with children and families, my answer would be unequivocal: "As parents, we are, unwittingly, too critical of our children."

This statement has surprised some of my colleagues and is at odds with much of the current conventional wisdom about contemporary parents—that we are overprotective or overly indulgent; or that we fail to provide our children with needed guidance and limits; or that we are too ready to be our child's friend, rather than an authority.

Research findings from many studies, however, now provide ample scientific evidence to support my personal experience and this, admittedly, anecdotal claim. Although it is at times difficult to distinguish cause and effect, clinical research consistently finds high levels of criticism—and fewer positive statements—in the interactions of parents and troubled children.[1]

We all know, from our own lives, how criticism feels. We may have experienced the demoralizing effect of frequent criticism in the workplace; or we may have suffered the eroding effect of frequent criticism on satisfaction in our love relationships. It is surprising, then, how often we fail to consider this in relation to our children. Persistent criticism breeds resentment and defiance, is destructive of a child's initiative and self-confidence, and undermines her motivation and sense of purpose. We need to prevent the buildup of these damaging attitudes in the minds of our children.

Research consistently shows high levels of criticism—and fewer positive statements—in the interactions of parents and troubled children.

Criticism from parents evokes in all children a complex emotional response. Every harsh criticism triggers some defiance as well as some demoralization and withdrawal. I have come to regard this sequence of events (with admitted exaggeration) as the psychological equivalent of Newton's Third Law: For every parental criticism there is an equal and opposite defiant reaction. As in physics, the nature of the opposing reaction (the child's defiant response) depends upon other forces that are present (the child's temperament and personality) and may not be openly expressed or immediately observable. Children may express their defiance at a later time, perhaps as defensiveness or argument, and then, increasingly, as resentment and grievance.

Many families are unaware of the presence of this toxin. Criticism has become part of the family atmosphere, either undetected or accepted as normal to those inside the family but often immediately apparent to an outside observer.

Many years ago, because no seats were available in nonsmoking cars, I was forced to sit in the smoking car of a commuter train. As I entered the car, a thick cloud of smoke was visible. After a short time, however, I no longer saw the pollution that was so apparent just a few minutes before; it was now "normal." When my eyes began to tear, I briefly wondered why this was happening. A toxin that had become invisible was, of course, still able to produce symptoms. This is what criticism is like in many families.

"My dad's a jerk." I have heard this statement far too often, said by children and adolescents about fathers who care deeply about their children and are deeply involved in their lives. Often, from my observations, it is not true. Why then, do so many children and adolescents feel this way?

The answer is that we do not realize how hurtful our words have been. When children respond poorly to criticism, with defensiveness or withdrawal, parents often say, "He is too sensitive." Perhaps. But we are all sensitive to criticism. And he may not be overly sensitive; rather, we may have been too critical and not sensitive enough.

The Criticism Paradox

Criticism is hurtful. Harsh, gratuitous, or persistent criticism is destructive, often deeply destructive, to parent–child relationships. Yet our ability to accept criticism, and to learn from criticism, is a hallmark of emotional maturity. Successful people, in all fields, seek ongoing criticism and instruction, even after they have achieved success.

At its best, criticism should encourage and guide self-improvement. In health, the criticisms we present to our children (and that others present to us) are absorbed or "metabolized" in a healthy way, in a way that strengthens us. Often, however, this is not the case. Our criticism becomes a toxin, linked to anger and resentment, and to a loss of motivation and initiative.

It seems necessary to ask, "Why are we so often critical of our children?" Much of our criticism is well intentioned, motivated by our desire for our children to improve, and eventually succeed, in a competitive world. In these instances, we criticize because we are anxious about our child's future. We regard our criticism as constructive, or not as criticism at all, but rather as instruction and advice.

Many parents feel justified in their criticism when they make an effort to balance criticism with praise. Because they are willing to offer praise for their child's good behavior, these parents do not regard themselves as critical. Other parents are aware of their criticalness. They believe, however, that it is their "right and responsibility" to be critical of their children, in order to prepare them for the demands and responsibilities they will face as adults. In giving this criticism, these parents believe that they are doing the right thing. They therefore continue to criticize, despite its bad effects.

From this perspective, shared by many of my colleagues, a child's defiance or withdrawal, or his unwillingness to communicate (especially in adolescence) is an unavoidable consequence of responsible parenting. I disagree. Of course, we must let children know of our disapproval, and all children can be expected to respond with some form protest when limits are set. Persistent criticism, however, damages our relationships with our children. And a "balance," or equal ratio, of praise and criticism has been shown to be unhealthy, both in marriage and in parent–child relationships.[2]

Too much criticism and instruction can also take the fun out of activities that children and adolescents would otherwise enjoy. Ask Andre Agassi.[3] Agassi's tennis instruction, described in his recent autobiography, *Open*, is, by any standard, extreme. When he was 7 years old, Andre hit 2,500 tennis balls a day. He became a great player, but he hated tennis.

For a far less extreme example, ask my son, Dan. The summer when Dan was 8, he and I looked forward, every evening, to having a baseball catch. This evening, Dan was not catching well. He was swatting at the ball with his glove and often missed. In an effort to help (but with some impatience), I offered the most basic baseball instruction: "Dan, catch with two hands." He frowned, ignored me, and continued to try to catch the ball the same way. When I repeated my instruction, he scowled; the third time, he became angry and tearful, and ran into the house.

Was he right, or was I? Was he stubborn and oversensitive? We both looked forward to this time together. Had he ruined it, or had I? There are no right answers to these questions; at least, I have not found any. But as I thought about this problem, I reminded myself, first, that he was 8 years old. He just wanted to have fun; there would be many other opportunities for instruction. At his next baseball practice, his coach would again show him the right way to catch a baseball, and he would listen. If he didn't, I would find another time, and another way, to teach him.

…hat was most important was for Dan and …g, to begin to repair our frustration and …and to think together about how to have …next day.

…al criticism is motivated by our anxiety (and our frustration) about our children's welfare, in the present and, especially, in the future. There are also deeper causes of persistent criticism, causes rooted in our character and life circumstances—how well we are able to cope with painful feelings in our own lives and how burdened we feel by the demands of raising our children. In my therapeutic work, I have found that parents who are critical of their children are often critical of each other, and less able to repair conflicts in their marriage and in their work relationships.

Often, however, we simply don't know another way.

Alternatives and Antidotes

We need a way out. We need to find alternatives and antidotes, to replace criticism and argument with understanding, appreciation, and problem solving. When frequent criticism persists, all other efforts to improve our family relationships are likely to fail.

Do we really need to criticize our children as often we do? Do we need, as some parents believe, to point out to a child every mistake he has made, every thing he has done wrong? Children almost always know when they have acted badly—because we have told them before. Our criticism just makes them defensive—*less* willing to accept responsibility for their actions and more preoccupied with defiant attitudes and inner argument.

Many parent advisors have offered sound advice on how to present criticism to children and mitigate its harmful effects. Earlier generations of parents were advised to make their criticisms specific, not global—to criticize a child's behavior, not his character (for example, we should not tell children that they are lazy, selfish, a failure, or that "you don't care about others") and to avoid the words "always" and "never." Parents have been advised to phrase criticisms as "I-messages" (to say, "I feel . . . when" instead of "You never . . .") and to present criticism in the form of a sandwich. In a criticism sandwich, we begin by recognizing a child's effort. Then, we offer criticism or instruction. Then, we express confidence in his ability to make improvements, to do better the next time. Isn't this how we would all like to hear criticism?[4]

Children almost always know when they have acted badly—because we have told them before.

All of this is sound advice. But it does not go far enough. Small but repeated criticisms of a child's behavior have an insidious harmful effect. When parents are often critical, even about minor matters, children begin to roll their eyes, and then we become furious at them for these expressions of disrespect.

The Importance of Patient Listening

The antidotes to criticism—simple in theory, but at times difficult in practice—are patient listening, recognition and praise for a child's efforts, and a proactive approach to resolving recurrent problematic situations.

The solution to the problem of persistent criticism begins with this fundamental fact: *Children, when they are not angry and discouraged, want to do well.* Your children want to earn your praise and approval, and they want you to be proud of them. Even parent advisors who believe (wrongly) that children are "lazy" or "little manipulators" recognize that, fundamentally, children seek a feeling of acceptance and belonging—and, I would add, a feeling of authentic pride.

There is no better antidote for frequent criticism and argument—and no better way to help children bounce back from the common frustrations and disappointments of childhood—than patient and respectful listening. Listening, of course, does not mean agreement or giving in to unreasonable demands. When we listen, we make a genuine effort to understand and appreciate our child's point of view and to acknowledge what is *right* about what he is saying before we point out what is *wrong*.

Our job is to listen. Listening requires patience. And patience requires time. When we are angry or critical of our children, it is almost always because we have lost patience with them. We cannot listen patiently when we are tired or hurried, or when we are trying to get things done. Our children, in healthy development, should come to understand this. We therefore need to set aside a special time to listen to our children.

Ten Minutes at Bedtime

I recommend that parents create moments, on a regular basis, that are conducive to this kind of patient listening. I encourage parents to set aside some extra time, perhaps 10 minutes at bedtime, for kids and parents to have a chance to talk. In these brief daily conversations, we should encourage kids to talk about whatever they were upset or angry about during the day, to say what they liked (or didn't like), or what they may be anxious about the following day. When they have nothing to talk about, we can make use of this opportunity to talk about the events of *our* day, perhaps to share a moment of frustration or a moment of humor.

Children look forward to these moments, just as they do opportunities for play. It is again surprising how infrequently we make this a regular part of a child's day. Often, when parents put aside time to listen and talk with their children, they report immediate improvement in their child's mood and behavior.

These are also times when you may be able to *initiate repair*. In every family, parents—especially when we are anxious and frustrated—will become critical and may say hurtful things to their children. At these times, it is important for us to take the lead and begin to repair these hurtful interactions. Moments of repair are of inestimable importance in our relationships with our children—and vital to their emotional health.

Often, when parents put aside time to listen and talk with their children, they report immediate improvement in their child's mood and behavior.

I encourage parents to find a time when their child is likely to be receptive, and then, to take responsibility for their own emotional responses. Reestablish dialogue, acknowledge your errors, and, when appropriate, apologize to your child. We should say, for example, "I know I was very angry at you earlier. Maybe I got *too* angry." Make some effort to appreciate, or at least acknowledge, your child's point of view. You can say, for example, "I know you really wanted to . . ."

Some parents express concern that, in apologizing to their children, they may implicitly condone their child's disrespectful or defiant behavior and diminish their authority as parents. This fear is understandable, but unfounded. Your apology does not excuse your child's bad behavior. ("You still should not have hit your sister.") To understand your child's mood is not to indulge his mood; the needs of others always have to be considered. In my opinion, when a parent initiates repair and offers an apology, he has modeled an important lesson in interpersonal relationships and *gains* authority with his child, because our children's acceptance of adult authority is, ultimately, based on respect.

"It's Not Fair!": Addressing Children's Grievances

When I talk with children who are angry, withdrawn, or behaving badly, many of them tell me about a grievance. They tell me, especially, about things in their life that are "not fair." His teachers are too strict or "mean"; or his parents yell at him, or punish him, but do not punish his siblings. He may complain about what he is not allowed to do, that he is not given any freedom; or about social cliques at school and being left out; that he is blamed for everything; that his parents are "always angry"; and, especially, that "no one listens" to him.

While we should certainly not take at face value everything our children tell us, it is still instructive how frequently kids complain that no one listens to them. We all know, of course, the experience of not being heard, how we feel when someone is not listening: We become angry; our voices get louder, more insistent, and more certain; we may exaggerate or become stubborn, even self-righteous. This is true for all of us, children no less than adults.

Children who are chronically "not heard" become increasingly demoralized and defiant. They may also become secretive and withdrawn, and they will look elsewhere for acceptance and understanding.

As parents, of course, we may also have grievances. We are often certain that we are right and that our child must change; if we are critical, it is because "he has to learn . . ." These impasses in family relationships are a frequent source of conflict and distress in contemporary families, painful to both parents and children. To solve them, we need to understand that both we and our children have legitimate concerns. In therapeutic work, I most often agree with parents' goals but suggest a different means of getting there.

A Lesson on Listening

It is not always easy for parents (or for child therapists) to "hear" a defiant child (or a cynical adolescent). A child's stated grievance, especially when it is expressed as a demand for "things," may mask a deeper unhappiness that he cannot yet talk about. And, of course, what he tells us may not be the whole story.

Arguing with your children will, in all likelihood, just make them better at arguing.

But when you are able to listen patiently, you will often find some truth in her side of the story—not only anger and blaming of others but also some previously unnoticed provocation or hurt feeling. More often than not, kids know when their demands are unreasonable and even that some punishment is called for. They are stuck, however, in their argument, justifying their actions. They have already heard criticism, judgment, and advice; now, they want you to "just listen"—so they can let go of the argument. And no matter how adamant or vociferous their defense ("He started it"), arguing with them will, in all likelihood, just make them better at arguing—more defiant in their attitudes and ɔborn in their self-defense. The more extensive this pro- ɔecome, the more difficult our empathic listening will ıe more patience will be required.

Understanding your child's grievance will also be easier when you realize that she has almost always made some effort in the direction of accommodating your requests, a small gesture toward cooperation or compromise. Often, however, her effort has gone unnoticed (or is "not enough"), hardening her grievance. When you are able to recognize and appreciate these small gestures, you begin to reverse a stubborn impasse.

Children are not always as demanding and unreasonable as they sometimes seem to be. Although they may repeatedly blame others, they do not always believe everything they say. Children know that they cannot get everything they want, and that their parents should not give in to all of their demands. All children (and most adolescents), except in the midst of an ongoing argument, acknowledge the need for rules and limits. It is commonly said that defiant children are "asking for limits" and there is, perhaps, some truth in this idea. More fundamentally, however, these children are asking to be heard; and they are willing, when their legitimate needs and concerns have been acknowledged, to accept some limit on their demands.

Your children do not expect you to agree but to listen.

When listening to your child, I therefore encourage you to *simply listen*; discussion and disagreement can come later. Optimally, you should listen with modesty and respect (you should say, for example, "I want to understand better how you feel") and with a genuine desire to find ways to alleviate your child's frustration and disappointment. And it is important to give your child time; try not, at that moment, to insist on a response. Many experienced therapists have noted that this may be especially important for boys, who often need more time to let go of their reflexive defensiveness.

Empathy

For those of us engaged … listening remains our … is universally acknow… psychotherapy. It is … relationships.

Empathy is no… gence. Empathy … maturity, and the esse… When you listen with empathy, … to put aside criticism and judgment and … feelings and her point of view. This effort—to ac… child's disappointments, frustrations, and hurt feelings, … hear her side of the story—confers unique and essential benefits in the emotional life of every child.

Empathy is more than being child friendly or "nice" to children (although it is that) and more than helping a child "feel better" (although it does that). Listening with empathy helps children bounce back. The solution of every emotional or behavioral problem of childhood should begin (but does not end) with your willingness to make a genuine effort to hear your child's concerns and to understand her point of view.

In moments of empathic understanding, as we all know from personal experience, our anger subsides, and our sadness and shame are attenuated. When you listen empathically to your children, they experience reduced stress—and then, increased cognitive and emotional flexibility. In your child's behavior, you will see less argument, less defiance, and less withdrawal.

These moments of empathic understanding then o… a pathway toward emotional maturity. Children become, i… increments, more open to compromise and proble…

In this way, your empat… in your child's attitud… fulcrum shift in a c… away from urgen… for disappoint… sonal respon…

The Li…

But …

r…

ny will help bring about a decisive change
es and behavior, what I described earlier as a
hild's emotional development—a movement
t and insistent demands and toward tolerance
ments and frustrations, and acceptance of per-
sibility.

mits of Empathy

is empathy always possible? And is it enough? Is an *empathic* esponse always the *right* response? If empathy is not indulgence, how can we tell the difference? How do we know when our sympathy for a child's feelings really has gone too far?

> **When you listen with empathy, children experience reduced stress and increased cognitive and emotional flexibility.**

The answer, I believe, is this: We always insist, no matter what our child's feelings—no matter how aggrieved or how hurt, no matter how unfair he feels we have been, or how badly he has been provoked—on limits to physical and verbal aggression.[5]

Teach your child the importance not only of his feelings but also the feelings of others, and insist on the rights of others. Insist on sharing—the first moral dilemma of childhood[6]—and on limits to buying. And put into practice the principle of earning. Our love and concern are unconditional, but privileges must be earned. (I will discuss how to implement the principle of earning in Chapter 9.)

Children also need to learn that there are many situations—
pecially situations of safety and when it is essential to get
done—when empathic responses are not the right

Empathy

For those of us engaged in therapeutic work, the art of empathic listening remains our most fundamental clinical skill. Empathy is universally acknowledged as a necessary requirement for all psychotherapy. It is also a necessity for healthy parent–child relationships.

Empathy is not hovering, not protectiveness, and not indulgence. Empathy is a basic human need, a nutrient of emotional maturity, and the essential component of all emotional healing. When you listen with empathy, you are making a deliberate effort to put aside criticism and judgment and to appreciate your child's feelings and her point of view. This effort—to acknowledge your child's disappointments, frustrations, and hurt feelings, and to hear her side of the story—confers unique and essential benefits in the emotional life of every child.

Empathy is more than being child friendly or "nice" to children (although it is that) and more than helping a child "feel better" (although it does that). Listening with empathy helps children bounce back. The solution of every emotional or behavioral problem of childhood should begin (but does not end) with your willingness to make a genuine effort to hear your child's concerns and to understand her point of view.

In moments of empathic understanding, as we all know from personal experience, our anger subsides, and our sadness and shame are attenuated. When you listen empathically to your children, they experience reduced stress—and then, increased cognitive and emotional flexibility. In your child's behavior, you will see less argument, less defiance, and less withdrawal.

These moments of empathic understanding then open a pathway toward emotional maturity. Children become, in small increments, more open to compromise and problem solving.

In this way, your empathy will help bring about a decisive change in your child's attitudes and behavior, what I described earlier as a fulcrum shift in a child's emotional development—a movement away from urgent and insistent demands and toward tolerance for disappointments and frustrations, and acceptance of personal responsibility.

The Limits of Empathy

But is empathy always possible? And is it enough? Is an *empathic* response always the *right* response? If empathy is not indulgence, how can we tell the difference? How do we know when our sympathy for a child's feelings really has gone too far?

When you listen with empathy, children experience reduced stress and increased cognitive and emotional flexibility.

The answer, I believe, is this: We always insist, no matter what our child's feelings—no matter how aggrieved or how hurt, no matter how unfair he feels we have been, or how badly he has been provoked—on limits to physical and verbal aggression.[5] Teach your child the importance not only of his feelings but also the feelings of others, and insist on the rights of others. Insist on sharing—the first moral dilemma of childhood[6]—and on limits to buying. And put into practice the principle of earning. Our love and concern are unconditional, but privileges must be earned. (I will discuss how to implement the principle of earning in Chapter 9.)

Children also need to learn that there are many situations—especially situations of safety and when it is essential to get things done—when empathic responses are *not* the right responses and your child's feelings do not count. In these instances, what matters is her behavior and its consequences.

For all of us, recognizing the limits of empathy is another essential aspect of emotional maturity. The world will not always be forgiving, and we do not always get a second chance. Children need to be taught that they must sometimes put aside their own needs and feelings; at this moment, what matters are the needs of others.

Empathy Is Not Indulgence

It is a misunderstanding, a myth, that a parent's effort to appreciate her child's point of view is indulgent, and that this "indulgence" causes children to become self-centered and demanding. The opposite is true. Children respond to our interest in their projects and our support for their concerns not with an attitude of entitlement but with *gratitude*.

Will empathic parents be more likely to indulge their children—to give in more often than they should to their child's requests or demands? Perhaps. It is true, when you make a sincere effort to understand your child's (or your spouse's or colleague's) point of view, you will be more likely to compromise, to find some way to accommodate her desires or concerns, even to give in (a little). This is because it is in the nature of empathy to be *influenced* by the other person, to be less sure, for example, that we are "right." Which is why listening with empathy is also essential to successful marriages.

Yes, there may be excesses. But we can always remain firm on our limits—on the need for safety and the rights of others. We can always say, "I understand that you are angry (or upset) but you must still talk to me calmly" or "I know you are disappointed, but it is still time to leave."

Empathy Is Not Easy

Empathy is often difficult. To remain empathic—noncritical and nonjudgmental—in the midst of a child's angry protest or stubborn refusal requires effort and resolve, and is hardly an easy task. How can we be empathic when a child is lying (or not telling the whole story), refuses to cooperate with basic tasks, denies any bad feelings, or acts in a hurtful or dangerously aggressive manner? Empathy is especially difficult when children are blaming others—it was the umpire who was wrong, her teacher who was unfair, or her sister who "started it"; when a child tells us that it's everyone else's fault, that she didn't do anything wrong, and she should not have been punished.

At these times, it is helpful to remember that we all do this, throughout our lives. We instinctively protect ourselves and blame others. How quickly we are able to get unstuck from blaming and acknowledge our errors may be yet another measure of our own emotional maturity.

At the end of the day, we have no substitute for, and no better "technique" to repair painful feelings and help children bounce back, than patient listening. Often, this is all that is necessary. In therapy, I know that I have been successful when a child tells me, "I don't have to come here anymore. Now I'm having good talks with my mom."

Chapter 6

The Character of Our Children

Most parents want more for their children than individual achievement. Of course, we want our children to do well and to go into the world with self-confidence and self-esteem. But we also want them to be "good kids"—children who act with kindness and generosity toward their families, their friends, and their communities.

Every family, and every society, has the task of socializing its children. Children need to learn to control their aggression, to play by the rules, and to be able to make and keep friends. We want our children to learn the importance of practice and hard work; to persevere, even when they are frustrated or discouraged; to develop and hone what psychologists now refer to as "executive skills"—the ability to organize their thoughts and control their impulses, to plan and carry out reasoned, and reasonable, actions. We want them to learn to "be prepared," to respect and help others, to understand and value their responsibilities as citizens.

How can we best accomplish these goals? In this chapter, I will discuss four essential processes of children's social and moral development: emotion regulation, interactive play, the maintenance of ideals, and the importance of doing for others.

Emotion Regulation

A consensus has emerged among contemporary child therapists. Persistent behavior problems in childhood and adolescence are increasingly understood as problems of "emotion regulation." Therapeutic programs to treat these problems all attempt, in different ways, to foster the development of improved emotion-regulation skills.[1]

Emotion regulation is an important idea with an unfortunate name. When we help children develop improved emotion regulation, we do not simply help them turn down the dial on their feelings or learn better anger management. (Yes, at times we will need to teach them—and to insist—that if they want to speak with us about a problem, they must speak to us calmly.) But emotion regulation is much more than anger management.

Children learn to express their emotions in constructive ways when they are confident that their feelings will be heard. When a child expects that her concerns will be appreciated and understood, her emotions become less urgent. Because each frustration and each disappointment now feels less painful, less "catastrophic," she will be less insistent in her demands, and more open and flexible in seeking solutions to problems.

Every advance in a child's ability to regulate her emotions—her ability to feel sad, anxious, or angry without withdrawal or impulsive action, and without making unreasonable demands—will also result in improved social adjustment. She will be better able to focus her attention, in school and on her homework, and she will resolve conflicts more easily with her friends. She will less often get stuck in attitudes of blaming, argument, and denial. She will be more able to feel empathy and concern for others, and to take responsibility for her actions.

These essential aspects of social maturity do *not* develop well in the presence of intense negative emotions. When children are often anxious, angry, or ashamed, they can usually focus only on their own painful feelings. They will be far less likely to think of the needs of others.[2]

Play

There is a second important pathway toward social maturity in children that also has scientific support: Young children learn essential social skills—cooperation, reciprocity, and the inhibition of aggressive behavior—in the context of pleasurable, interactive play—especially when they play (and work) with their parents. In many respects, interactive play is to children's social development what talking with children is to their vocabulary development and what exercise is to their physical development.

Interactive play is to children's social development what talking with children is to their vocabulary development and what exercise is to their physical development.

Those of us who work with children learn yet another elementary lesson from our daily therapeutic interactions: Children want to playfully engage with admired adults who respond with enthusiasm to their interests and emerging skills, and who join in the play. In the course of this play, children learn—deeply and for the right reasons—to accept the limitations imposed by adult authority. They must play by the rules so that the game can go on.

The Neuroscience of Play

For many years, play has been regarded as the primary expressive medium for young children. A child's play, it has been thought, is the equivalent of an adult's free associations—an undisguised expression of children's feelings and fantasies. And it remains true; in their play, children often reveal feelings they have held back, unable to more openly express.

Children's play, however, is much more than an expression of wishes and fantasies. We now know that play is essential to children's intellectual and social development.[3] Every moment of interactive play, especially play with an admired adult, offers opportunities for children to learn and practice important social skills. Your child is learning, through experience, the limits of verbal and physical aggression and the need to make accommodations to others—that she cannot, for example, push too hard and must wait her turn.

Neuroscientist Jaak Panksepp argues that play is an instinctive behavior in mammals, and that the basic brain structures that promote play are shared by all mammals. Panksepp notes that when animals are housed in isolation, they become hungry for play. The hallmark expression of play (in both humans and other mammals) is *laughter*. This emotional expression seems to have evolved as a social signal—a signal of victory, group solidarity, or safety.[4]

In rats, play has been demonstrated to activate areas of the brain involved in social development. Panksepp has also found evidence (again, in rats) that abundant opportunities for play may reduce, to some extent, the impulsive behavior that results from damage to the brain's frontal lobes.[5] He offers the intriguing hypothesis that, in children, an impoverishment of play and playfulness may intensify a child's materialism (and, I would add, a child's demandingness)—that children often ask for "things" as substitutes for playful interactions.

Reciprocity

A generation ago, child psychologists Mary Parpal and Eleanor Maccoby designed a simple but important study to better understand how young children develop cooperative behavior. In this study, mothers were asked to play with their 3- to 4-year-old children for 10–15 minutes each night. During the play period, children were allowed to choose any activity and to control the nature and rules of the interaction. Mothers were instructed not to praise their children "but rather, to participate positively in the child's play . . . to describe and imitate her child's behavior, to comply with her child's directives . . . [and] to let the child know that she enjoyed playing."

This brief training in responsive play was highly effective. Just 1 week later, children in this group were more willing than other children to comply with their parents' requests. Responsive play also seemed to have had its greatest effect on "difficult" or hyperactive children.[6]

Tools of the Mind

More recently, the remarkable success of the Tools of the Mind curriculum for preschool and kindergarten children, developed by Elena Bedrova and Deborah Leong, provides additional evidence for the importance of play in children's intellectual and behavioral development. In the Tools curriculum, children first plan and then engage in long interactive play scenarios. In studies across the country, children in Tools classrooms made great advances, in short periods of time, on tests of cognitive development, executive functioning, and academic achievement.[7]

Children in these classrooms also showed almost none of the distracted and disruptive behavior that is so common in most schools—and in non-Tools classrooms in the same schools. In their book *Nurture Shock*, Po Bronson and Ashley Merryman report, for example, that "after just three months . . . Tools teachers in New Mexico went from averaging forty reported classroom incidents a month to zero . . . During one lunch period in a New Jersey school cafeteria, the Tools kindergarteners watched the entire rest of the student body become embroiled in a food fight. Not one Tools kid picked up as much as a scrap of food to throw."[8]

If we want our children to be well behaved and to play (and work) well with others, we should play (and work) with them often.

The implications of this research for how we can promote our children's social development is clear: If we want our children to be well behaved—to cooperate, to control their aggression, and to play (and work) well with others—we should play (and work) with them often.

The Social Benefits of Play

Consider the many benefits of interactive play between parents and children:

- Interactive play provides opportunities for shared positive emotions—emotions of interest and excitement, and expressions of pride in children's accomplishments.
- Interactive play provides opportunities for children to learn accommodation and reciprocity. In play, accommodation to the other person is always necessary and learned experientially.
- Moments of anxiety, frustration, and disappointment inevitably occur in the course of interactive play. This is true of fantasy play and, especially, of structured games: a toy is broken or missing; a tower accidentally falls; the

child's spin or roll of the dice does not land her on the space that she wants. These are teachable moments (although better taught by example than by even gentle lectures). When parents talk with children about their frustration and disappointment, and offer solace and consolation, children develop some increment in their tolerance for frustration and some measure of emotional and behavioral flexibility, and problem solving.

- Interactive play provides opportunities for controlled and softened expressions of defiance and aggression, for example, teasing.[9]
- Adult play with children provides continual opportunities for kids to learn rules and limits. Every playful interaction necessarily involves some subtle limit or prohibition. If we are playing catch, neither player can throw too hard; in play fighting, a child cannot hurt her opponent. In these interactions, children come to understand that rules are necessary—for safety and for living with others. These socializing influences do not occur in solitary play. In our homes and in every group activity, this is how children learn to accept rules and limits—from experience, in the context of intrinsically rewarding play.

It is important to note that this is not learning through instruction. To the dismay of many well-intentioned parents, most children do not learn good behavior from repeated talks or lectures. Adult intervention is effective because the rule must be observed *in order to continue the play*.

Ideals

Even this important research, however, does not give us a full picture of children's social and moral development.

Our children look up to us. A young child's idealization of his or her parents, and of older children, is one of the most readily observable facts of childhood. The young child believes that her parents know everything and can do anything. Our children regard our accomplishments, large and small, with a kind of awe that is difficult to recapture in adult life.

It is easy to overlook this essential aspect of childhood, especially when children are acting badly. But our children look up to us even when they are angry and defiant, or when they are defensive or withdrawn, and even when, as adolescents (or before), they challenge our ideas and rebel against our rules.

Because they look up to you, they want to be, and to become, like you. They want to be as strong (or stronger) than you are, to do what you are able to do, to know as much as you know, and to be looked up to by others. Children derive an almost ineffable feeling of inner strength and well–being from these experiences of idealization, from being in the presence of admired adults.

We all know this, of course. We can observe it, every day, in the admiring statements of young children: When first-grade boys and girls tell their teacher, "I want to be a fireman like my daddy," or "I want to be a doctor and help people, like my mom." Or when an 8-year-old boy writes a card to his grandfather, "Grandpa, please get well. You are a king to me."[10]

Our children's wanting to be like us is an essential motivating influence throughout childhood—a source of conscience, of ideals, and of long-term goals. When a child looks up to us—and in return, feels our genuine interest, warmth, and pride—we have strengthened an essential pathway of healthy emotional development, a pathway that leads toward commitment and ideals, and becomes a foundation for a child's sense of purpose.

When neuroscientists find a way to study this emotional experience, I believe they will find, at these moments, that a child's brain lights up in a unique and important way. In the meantime, we may not be able to see it in their brains, but we can see it in their eyes.[11]

Disillusionment

Inevitably, we will disillusion them. Especially in adolescence, they will become aware of our failings; we cannot sustain the awe of early childhood. They will see that we do not know as much as they once assumed we did, and that we do not always live up to the values we espouse. Disillusionment is painful, but unavoidable, for both parents and children.

I was fortunate, in growing up, to have parents who I continued to admire and respect. Still, I can recall, from both sides, as a son and as a parent, the painfulness of adolescent disillusionment.

We disillusion our children especially when we are frequently angry and critical—with our children or with each other—and when we are unavailable to offer encouragement and support. If we disillusion our children profoundly, we will have damaged an important source of motivation. They will turn away from us and away from long-term goals.[12]

I have talked with too many deeply disillusioned children and adolescents. They are not doing well in their lives. They do not need more frequent rewards or more consistent punishments. And they do not need greater expectations, because they will not be able to live up to them.

Many years ago, I asked a 10-year-old boy who loved baseball whether his father was able to come to any of his Little League games. Sadly, this young boy had already correctly observed his father's character. He answered, with precocious cynicism and resentment, "My father will leave work early for an appointment with a contractor, but not to come to one of my baseball games." This boy was already deeply disillusioned. It is likely that he will be hindered in his ability to pursue constructive goals, and that any effort by his father to command respect will have, at best, superficial success.

In moments of anxiety and self-doubt, we turn to others.[13] When our children are unsure about whether they can compete and succeed, or when they are unsure about what is the right thing to do, they will look to us, throughout life. When we have disillusioned them, we are no longer available to fill this need. Their anxieties and their self-doubt will feel more urgent. They will experience more stress (both emotional and physical) and they will be less able to moderate their frustration and anger.

As parents, we also continue to look to others (especially our own parents) for affirmation and support, when we are unsure about whether we are doing the right thing for our children. If we expect criticism, or lack of interest, or lack of support, we are also more likely to become demoralized and angry.

Idealism

Children are idealistic. In health, some of this idealism should remain. Ideals are the positive side of conscience; they make learning relevant and meaningful. Cynicism and disillusionment are bad for our health and bad for our children.

Ideals are the positive side of conscience; they make learning relevant and meaningful.

We want our children to remain idealistic. We read them stories about heroes we hope will inspire them and preserve their ideals. We read to them about Jackie Robinson, about Rosa Parks and Martin Luther King, Jr.; Eleanor Roosevelt and Dwight Eisenhower; Jonas Salk and the Dalai Lama. When we celebrate their graduations, we again attempt to inspire them. We bestow honorary degrees on scientists, artists, scholars, and political leaders whose lives we hope will continue to motivate them to pursue careers of leadership and service.

Our children's respect for us is the ultimate source of our authority and influence. When we are no longer admired or respected, we no longer have any lasting influence. When we have only the power to punish, our attempts to set limits on our children's behavior, and to teach them to use good judgment and make good decisions, will have only a short-lived effect. They will be defiant when they can get away with it, and then we will become angrier and more disappointed in them.

Doing for Others

A growing body of scientific research now supports the following important conclusion: Doing good for others is good for us. Most of this research has been done with late adolescents and adults. My personal experience suggests that doing for others is also good for children.

Martin Seligman conducted an informal experiment with his college students. For these students, performing small acts of kindness and philanthropy—especially when these acts engaged the students' personal strengths and virtues—resulted in far more personal gratification and happiness than activities that were simply pleasurable. Seligman reports that this simple experiment was a life-changing experience for many of his students.[14]

In a recent review, psychologist Jane Piliavin concluded that community service—helping others as part of an institutional framework—leads to improved self-esteem, less frequent depression, better immune system functioning, even a longer life. We will learn more, in the coming years, about the mechanisms that underlie these health benefits and about the exact conditions that make them more or less likely to occur. In the meantime, it is hard to argue with these results.

Piliavin found significant benefits, for example, when older elementary school students read to kindergartners or first graders. Good effects (including lower dropout rates) were also reported when middle school students were randomly assigned to tutor younger children, as little as 1 hour a week. An evaluation of student volunteering that involved 237 different locations and almost 4,000 students concluded that volunteering "led to increased intrinsic work values, the perceived importance of a career, and the importance of community involvement."[15]

Finally, research published in 2008 in the journal *Science* demonstrated that spending money on others (prosocial spending) leads to increased happiness, whereas spending money on ourselves (personal spending) does not. In one study, spending as little as $5 on others led to a measurable increase in happiness.[16]

My clinical experience is consistent with these experimental results. I therefore now recommend that parents find some way, especially as a family, to make doing for others a regular, not just occasional, part of their children's lives. Children learn from this work that they have something to offer and they experience the appreciation of others. They learn how good it feels, to themselves and to others, to do good work.

Caring Children

For several decades, behaviorist principles—principles of reward and punishment—have been dominant in our understanding of children's moral development. In this theory, children learn moral behavior because they are rewarded (with praise, approval, or more tangible rewards) for doing what is right, and because they are punished for doing what is wrong.

This basic principle is widely accepted. Many parents believe that this is how children learn responsible behavior—that children learn from the consequences of their actions. And this is the advice most commonly offered to parents, by therapists and in the public media: Be consistent in the rules you establish and in the consequences you impose.[17]

There is, of course, some self-evident truth in this idea. It is true, we all learn from the consequences of our actions. All of us, at times, will regulate our behavior because of the consequences that will follow, and our ability to do this—to foresee consequences and act accordingly—is another essential aspect of emotional maturity.

But there are also limitations to the behaviorist approach.

Most parents want more than this. We want more than our child's acceptance of adult authority and compliance with adult demands. We hope to nurture in our children feelings of empathy and concern for others, of appreciation and gratitude, and a desire for giving, not simply getting. And these goals are not accomplished by any system of rewards and punishments.

We hope to nurture in our children feelings of empathy and concern for others, of appreciation and gratitude, and a desire for giving, not simply getting.

Several decades of research support the conclusion that moral development in childhood depends less on a child's fear of punishment and far more on a "good socializing relationship"[18]—a parent–child relationship characterized by secure attachment, parental warmth, and responsiveness to children's needs—and the learning of reciprocity.[19]

In a series of studies conducted by psychologist Ross Thompson and his colleagues, for example, frequent references to rules and consequences were not the most effective means of fostering moral understanding and prosocial behavior in young children. Instead, children's prosocial behavior depended on shared positive feelings between parents and children and a mother's use of emotion language in conversation with her child. In these studies, mothers of children who were high in conscience used what Thompson labeled an "elaborative" conversational style, in which they made frequent references to other people's feelings. [20]

Several years ago, psychologists Nancy Eisenberg and Paul Mussen presented a comprehensive review of research on the development of prosocial behavior—caring, sharing, and helping behaviors—in children. They concluded that prosocial behavior begins with a child's empathy—his awareness of the feelings of others—and is then strengthened through the observation of admired adults and older children. Concern for others does not develop primarily through moral teaching or from rewards for moral behavior. Moral development, it appears, can be refined, but not created, by moral instruction.

Observation of admired adults is clearly important in the development of caring behavior. For young boys, their relationship with their father may be especially important. In one study, preschool boys who were generous toward other children portrayed their fathers as "nurturant and warm, as well as generous, sympathetic, and compassionate, whereas boys low in generosity seldom perceived their fathers in these ways."

Parents often attempt to promote respectful behavior in their children by repeated lecturing. This is rarely, if ever, effective. Across cultures, however, children who are given family responsibilities, including household chores and teaching younger children, show more helpful and supportive behavior toward their families and their peers.

Harsh discipline seems to *inhibit* the development of prosocial behavior, and abusive treatment *prevents* the expression of caring behavior in young children. Children whose parents are described as authoritarian and punitive generally show low levels of socially responsible behavior. In one study, *no abused child ever* showed concern, sadness, or empathy for other children.

Eisenberg and Mussen cite a study of non-Jews who had risked their lives to rescue Jews from the Nazis during World War II. A composite portrait emerged of the early development of these rescuers, a portrait that Eisenberg and Mussen note is highly consistent with other studies of people who engage in altruistic behavior:

> It begins in close family relationships in which parents model caring behavior and communicate caring values. Parental discipline tends toward leniency; children frequently experience it as almost imperceptible. It includes a heavy dose of reasoning—explanations of why behaviors are inappropriate, often with reference to their consequences for others. Physical punishment is rare . . . parents set high standards for their children, particularly with regard to caring for others. They implicitly or explicitly communicate the obligation to help others in a spirit of generosity. Parents themselves model such behaviors, not only in relation to their children but also toward other family members and neighbors.

This study supports the importance of high standards for our children's moral behavior, but it challenges the idea that children need more firm discipline.[21]

We cannot predict all of the challenges and moral dilemmas our children will encounter in the course of their lives. We can only prepare them, as best we can, with a foundation. And the foundation of our children's character is built on understanding their feelings—and on helping them understand the feelings of others.

Chapter 7

Putting It All Together

In this chapter, I will offer practical recommendations—things that we can do with our children on a daily basis—to strengthen our family relationships and foster our children's emotional health.

Many of these ideas have been discussed in the preceding chapters in a more general way. Some of the advice I will offer is simple and timeless but often lost in the pace and stress of modern life; most of these recommendations now have the support of scientific research. Above all, this is the advice that has been most helpful, over many years, to the families I have worked with in my clinical practice.

How Can We Be More Positive With Our Children?

Express enthusiastic interest in your child's interests.

Find out what arouses their interest and become interested in it. Be animated and enthusiastic. Ask them about their collections—their cards and their dolls. Find out about the athletes and celebrities they admire.

Hang out with them.

Support their projects. All the highly "purposeful" adolescents and young adults in William Damon's recent study—highly motivated and effective young people with passionate commitments to music, technological innovation, religious, political, and altruistic causes—had the enthusiastic support of their family, mentors, and friends.[1]

If they are only interested in watching television or playing video games, watch and play with them. Ask them to teach you the game. I have never met any child who did not want to show (and tell) his parents about the video or computer games he liked to play.

Encouragement, encouragement, encouragement.

We learn, again, an elementary lesson, from both developmental research and from daily therapeutic work: Our children need our enthusiastic encouragement and support.[2]

In her book, *Mindset*, discussed in Chapter 1, Carol Dweck offers helpful insights into the qualities of outstanding teachers. Great teachers are deeply imbued with a growth mindset. They create an atmosphere of warmth and acceptance; they respond to the individual needs of each student; and they communicate a belief in their students' potential and joy in their progress. In this setting of encouragement and acceptance, it is possible to set very high expectations.

Dweck describes, for example, the teaching method of Dorothy DeLay, teacher of Itzak Perlman and other great violinists at the Julliard School. One of Delay's students described his instruction from Delay:

> We were working on my sound, and there was this one note I played, and Miss Delay stopped me and said, "Now *that* is a beautiful sound." She then explained how every note has to have a beautiful beginning, middle, and end, leading into the next note. And he thought, "Wow! If I can do it there, I can do it everywhere."[3]

These teachers should be role models for us, as parents.

Play with them, at every age.

If we want our children to be well behaved and to get along well with others, we should play (and work) with them often.

Essential social skills are learned in the course of playful interactions. They are not learned in front of a screen. They are not learned through repeated talks, lectures, or admonishments. And they are not learned in moments of defiance or moments of loneliness.

Every moment of interactive play with an admired adult is a moment of shared interest and enjoyment, and therefore beneficial in a child's emotional life. It is also a mini-lesson in coping with frustration and disappointment, in making accommodations and getting along with others, and in learning self-restraint.

When they are young, get down on the floor. Play with them when they play with their dolls, cars, and blocks; with their army men and action figures; and on their favorite Web sites. Play games of hiding, chase, and push down. Throw balls and build sand castles. Build block towers—and then knock them down. Make scribbles and then pictures. Get in the pool with them. It is much easier to be a supportive (and an "effective") parent when we are not watching from the sidelines.

Martin Seligman recommends that, beginning in infancy, parents play what he calls "synchrony games" with their children. In these games (which can be played at any time of the day) parents imitate a young child's actions. If your child, for example, bangs three times, you bang three times. Seligman believes that these "games" provide children with an early experience of mastery and of having an effect on another person. At the very least, all children enjoy these activities. They smile and want to do more.[4]

Take them hiking, fishing, and camping. Join their fantasy play. Play card games and board games. Find activities that require learning and doing together. Help restore parks and build playgrounds. One of the greatest changes in family life over the course of the 20th century has been the segregation of the work of children from the work of parents.

When you have work to do, "deputize" them. Find a way to allow them to participate in the work. Psychologist Lawrence Balter made this helpful recommendation many years ago, when my children were young.[5] If you are building a bookshelf or cooking a meal, let them take out their toy hammer or toy cooking utensils and build or cook with you.

Playful interactions with our children—the delight of parents, grandparents, and young children—often seem to fade when children enter school and we become, understandably, preoccupied with the development of their academic skills. This is unfortunate, however, because the play of children, especially interactive play, remains a primary source of creativity, problem solving, and the refinement of children's social skills.

Create more moments of "positive affect sharing."

Find out what they like and why they like it. Enjoy it with them. Find out what makes them laugh—and laugh with them.

Sing songs with them. Applaud their shows. Be charmed by their curiosity and exuberance. These are the "magic years,"[6] the age of illusion, and the age of fun.

Cultivate a "growth mindset" and a "language of becoming."

Focus on their strengths.

Respect their individuality. This is yet another, widely accepted, lesson of research in child development: Children differ in their temperaments. Children differ in their sensory thresholds, their activity level, and their inherent interests and skills. In school, we teach children that it is important to do well in all their classes. In life, however, our success depends much more on doing one thing well.

I recently learned that George Gershwin, as a young boy, was incorrigible, truant, and hyperactive—until he found music.[7] And, of course, so was Babe Ruth—until (and perhaps after) he found baseball.

Even children with significant learning problems demonstrate areas of competence, or qualities of character, that should be a source of inner pride and a foundation for their future success. These strengths need to be recognized and supported.

Let them know you are proud of them, not for their intelligence or their talents, but for their effort and for the good things they do for others.

All children want their parents to be proud of them—as parents want to be proud of their children. Expressions of pride and encouragement from admired adults evoke in children a unique—and essential—good feeling. This feeling is then internalized. Your pride in your children promotes their acceptance of adult authority and becomes a sustaining influence in moments of disappointment, discouragement, and temptation.

Tell them, "That was a really nice thing you did when you helped your friend (or sister, or brother)." For many years, parents have been advised to "Catch your child being good." This is sound advice, as far as it goes. We should always do this, in all our relationships.

Offer support in moments of frustration and disappointment.

Help them put their disappointments in perspective and find meaning in their *effort*, not only their success. None of us are good at everything; all of us have failed; we have all suffered rejection and disappointment. When the tower falls, we can rebuild it together.

When your children feel sad or angry, you should let them know that you know how they feel. "Yes, I know, it feels really bad when other kids won't let you play. . . I also felt bad and angry when those kinds of things happened to me." Many children will respond to these statements with astonishment. "That happened to you!?" And, of course, it has.

We should let our children know that we have also suffered frustrations and disappointments, and moments of embarrassment. We can then talk with them about how we have overcome our disappointments and tell them that we are confident that they will, too.

Optimism and resilience are not about avoiding disappointment and frustration, but about not giving up.

Use humor—but not sarcasm.

Be silly. All experienced child therapists know the value of humor in their work with children, in putting children at ease.

Much of our humor, probably more than we would like to admit, involves making fun of, laughing at someone, or putting someone down. When we are silly, we are making fun of ourselves. Our willingness to do this communicates safety, and we come down off our pedestal.

Sarcasm is not playful humor. Sarcasm (literally, "tearing flesh") communicates contempt and is deeply hurtful. Expressions of contempt (even nonverbal expressions of contempt) are among the most destructive forces in all our relationships and must be repaired.

Be generous with your praise.

Praise their effort, not their intelligence or innate ability, and praise their effort whether they succeed or fail. We are proud of them—not for winning but for trying. But do not be afraid of praise.

Generous praise does not create praise junkies. The opposite is true.

Praise is not, as some parent advisors have come to believe, like sugar—something we crave but is ultimately harmful to our health. It is a basic human need. Praise (and approval or appreciation) is more like oxygen or an essential nutrient, something that we cannot do without, or else we suffer symptoms of illness.

Contrary to the recommendations of some parent advisors, I believe that we should tell children that they have done a good job. Saying "good job" is not empty praise and it is not a method of behavioral control. It is an expression of appreciation. We need this affirmation. It sustains us when we are discouraged or angry.

Teach but don't lecture.

Lectures never help. For many children, the second sentence is already the beginning of a lecture. I recall giving important advice to my teenage daughter, who responded, "Dad, you've told me that 10 times." I was sure it was only the second time. When we offer instruction and advice, less is often more.

When you have to say, "No," don't just say, "No."

Do not make "No" your default option. When you have to say, "No," you can still acknowledge your child's disappointment and frustration. Explain (briefly) why you are saying, "No."

Then, whenever possible, offer an alternative, a "next time," or the possibility of your child earning what he wants. You can do this even in infancy. If your child is banging on the table, give him a drum.

Have frequent dinners together as a family.

The following summary of research from the National Center on Addiction and Substance Abuse (CASA) of Columbia University is important enough to quote at length:

> Over the past decade and a half of surveying thousands of American teens and their parents, we have discovered that one of the most effective ways parents can keep their kids from using substances is by sitting down to dinner with them . . . And it is also important for parents to give kids their undivided attention—and to get theirs . . . The message for parents could not be any clearer: turn off your cell phone (and tell your kids to do the same), and make a regular date with your kids. Let them know how important they are to you. Listen to what they have to say.[8]

Share personal stories.

There is no better way to engage a young child's attention and provide emotional support than with personal stories.

My experience with the benefits of telling personal stories has received some recent research support. Psychologists Marshall Duke and Robyn Fivush, along with their colleagues at the Center for Myth and Ritual in American Life of Emory University, have demonstrated the importance of storytelling as a way of promoting resilience in school-age children. In several studies, children's knowledge of their family history was strongly related to their general well-being and to a positive sense of self. (Children were asked, for example, "Do you know how your parents met?"; "Do you know where some of your grandparents grew up?") These researchers note, of course, that a child's knowledge itself is not what is healthy and protective in her emotional development; instead, her knowledge is a sign, and a result, of healthy family communication and family cohesiveness.[9]

Make a date for a special activity.

Get up early and have a special breakfast together.

Leave them notes.

If you leave for work before they are up, leave a note on the floor of their room or in their lunchbox.[10]

Smile at them and give them big hugs.

Research in both humans and other animals has demonstrated profound benefits from physical touch. "Human infants who receive little touching grow more slowly . . . Throughout life, they show larger reactions to stress, are more prone to depression, and are vulnerable to deficits in cognitive functions commonly seen in depression and during stress."

Therapeutic massage for infants can ameliorate these deficits. Infants treated with therapeutic massage, across cultures, gain weight and show improved cognition and reduced stress.[11]

Make note of increments of progress.

Acknowledge every small step on the road to success, of doing better today than the day before.

If your child is involved in organized sports, join the Positive Coaching Alliance.

Jim Thompson has developed an excellent philosophy and helpful techniques for coaching children in organized sports. Thompson's coaching recommendations have been endorsed by many professional athletes and coaches, including Phil Jackson, Herm Edwards, Doc Rivers, and Nadia Comaneci.

Thompson reminds us that professional sports and youth sports are fundamentally different enterprises. The goal of professional sports is winning. Youth sports have other, more important, goals. We want our children to play sports for enjoyment and to learn to value physical activity; and to help them learn, in Thompson's words, "to bounce back from difficulties with renewed determination" and to "discover how to support other people in a team context."

Winning, in Thompson's philosophy, is the "Little Picture." Character development is the "Big Picture." How often do we lose sight of the big picture? How often do we hear coaches (and parents) criticizing and yelling at young athletes?

Thompson believes (and I wholeheartedly agree) that children learn to bounce back when we fill their "emotional tanks" with appreciation, listening, encouragement, and praise for their effort. Too often, instead, we drain their emotional tanks with criticism and sarcasm. Too often, children become anxious, even paralyzed, by their fear of making a mistake, or drop out of sports because it is no longer fun.

Errors in the field, Thompson tells his players, are "no sweat." He suggests that parents and coaches use a "mistake ritual"—a gesture from the sideline (for example, two fingers across our forehead, indicating, "no sweat") that helps children wipe away their mistakes and reset on enjoying the game.

Of course, all children need instruction and criticism. Thompson understands, however, that children learn best during teachable moments—moments when they are receptive to instruction. (This is true not only in sports, but in everything we want to teach our children.) Some moments are not teachable. After a child makes an error or after his team loses a game is not the right moment; at these times, children will only become defensive.

Thompson recommends that coaches work to create teachable moments through "relentless positivity." For example, during every game or practice, Thompson advises coaches to jot down 3–5 positive things that each player does, and then to review these observations during a brief team meeting at the beginning of the next practice. (And he correctly adds that, if we look hard enough, we "will find positive things that each player does.")[12]

Be positive, be positive, be positive.

There is a frequently cited rule among people who sell real estate, that the value of any property is determined by three factors: location, location, and location. There is an equivalent rule, I believe, for fostering our children's emotional health: Be positive, be positive, be positive.

Listen for the great sound or creative idea.

Tell them, every night as they are going to bed, how much you love them.

Then ask them what they want to do for fun tomorrow, after school or after work. Make a plan together to do it. If there are responsibilities that must come first, let them know this and make a plan to do them.

We should ask ourselves, at the end of every day, have I been positive with my child—or teenager—today?

How Can We Repair Conflict and Misunderstanding With Our Children?

Set aside time—every day—to listen to their concerns.

We learn, again, an elementary lesson from therapeutic work with children and families: Our children will be more willing to listen to us when they feel that we have listened to them.

Our job is to listen. But we cannot listen patiently—or listen well—when we are tired or hurried; when we are burdened or preoccupied; when we are trying to get things done; or when, at that moment, we are just too angry. Our children, in healthy development, should come to understand this.

When we are angry or critical of our children, it is almost always because we have lost patience with them. We therefore need to create moments that are conducive to patient listening. At these times, we ask our child whether there is something she might want to talk about—perhaps a problem she is having at school, or with her friends, something she is angry with us about, or something she might "feel bad" about.

Children look forward to these moments, just as they do opportunities for play. Often, when we set aside time, on a regular basis, to listen and talk with our children, we see immediate improvement in their mood and behavior.

Initiate repair.

Make a deliberate effort to set aside criticism and judgment as long as you can and to appreciate your child's feelings and her point of view. Listen to your children's concerns. Acknowledge her disappointments, frustrations, and hurt feelings, and every small gesture she makes toward cooperation and compromise.

Hear her side of the story.

Don't stay angry.

Children learn invaluable lessons from moments of repair. They learn that, although it is not always easy, moments of anger and misunderstanding are *moments* and *can be repaired.*

This may be the most important lesson we can teach, the lesson that is most vital to our children's emotional health. Disappointments are disappointments. Bad feelings are not forever.

In moments of repair, children begin to develop a more balanced, less all-or-nothing, perspective on the disappointments and frustrations in their lives. They develop greater ability to bounce back from moments of sadness and anger; greater willingness to cooperate and appreciate the needs of others; and they are better able to get along with their peers. Moments of repair may also reduce a child's level of physiological stress.

When you need to criticize, criticize thoughtfully and gently.

Criticism is hurtful. Harsh, persistent, or gratuitous criticism is deeply destructive to our relationships with our children—and to our children's emotional health.

Children make mistakes. So do we.

Try to be gentle and tolerant in your response to their mistakes, and apologize for your own. Because we are anxious about our children's success, we are often more tolerant of *our* mistakes than of theirs. But if you are willing to acknowledge your mistakes, your children will more willingly acknowledge theirs.

The alternatives to criticism are simple in theory but difficult in practice: patient listening, recognition of your child's efforts, and a proactive approach to resolving recurrent problematic situations.

Present criticisms as a sandwich. Express confidence in your child's ability to make improvements. Acknowledge every increment of effort and success, even when these efforts fall far short of your goal. A "balance," or equal ratio, of praise and criticism is unhealthy, in marriage and in parent–child relationships.

Jim Thompson offers these additional recommendations for offering criticism to young athletes, what Thompson calls "kid-friendly criticism":

> Always criticize in private. Criticism in front of others causes embarrassment and is likely to make children angry, defensive, and stubborn.
>
> Children do not respond well to criticism if we criticize when we are angry.
>
> It is often helpful to "ask permission" when we offer criticism. We can say, for example, "Is it OK if I give you some advice about how you were playing today?" or "Are you open to hearing some criticism about how you played in today's game?" When introduced in this way, children will be much more receptive to what we have to say. Usually, they will say that they are ready to listen. If they say, "No," we should accept this and tell them, "OK. Maybe we can talk about it later" or "Let me know if you change your mind."

Thompson's recommendations are helpful and important, not only when children are playing sports but for all activities they are involved in and for our daily family lives.

Express appreciation.

Expressions of appreciation repair family relationships. Appreciation begins to unlock stubbornness. Criticism—and the resentment it creates—although necessary in small doses, is a toxin. Appreciation is the antidote for resentment.

Appreciate every effort on the part of your child at cooperation and concern for others. We should express appreciation to our children for the little things they do—for their cooperation and helpfulness, and for their gestures of concern for others (especially their siblings). Simple, genuine expressions of appreciation are often remarkably helpful in softening a child's intransigence and opening her to collaboration in solving problems. Isn't this true for all of us, in all our relationships?

Instead of argument, engage your child in problem solving.

Ask your child for her ideas. Seek common ground. Appreciate her concerns, then let her know yours.

When parents are angry and critical with their children, children, in turn, become angry and argumentative, stubborn and defiant. Argument begets argument. When we argue frequently with our children, children become good at arguing.

Instead of argument, engage your child in active problem solving. Regard your child's defiant behavior as a problem to be solved. (I will discuss problem solving in more detail in Chapter 8.)

Make an effort to understand what is important to them.

Then tell them what is important to you.

Tell them what is right about what they are saying or doing before you tell them what they are doing wrong.

Withhold your judgments as long as you can—and then a little longer.

Remember: Children, when they are not angry and discouraged, want to do well.

Your children want to earn your praise and approval, and they want you to be proud of them.

Remember: Children are not always as demanding and unreasonable as they sometimes seem to be.

Children almost always know when they have acted badly. If they have not practiced or studied hard enough, they already know this and already feel badly, whether or not they will admit this to us.

More often than not, children know when their demands are unreasonable and even when some punishment is called for. Instead of criticism, express confidence that they will do better the next time. You can then ask, "Do you think there's a way that I might be able to help?"

Give them time.

In talking with children about any difficult problem, do not insist on an immediate response. Even minor criticisms evoke defensiveness in most children; a defensive wall quickly comes up. Children need time to think about, and eventually accept, our instruction and advice. When you bring up a problem, place the problem before your child, ask her to think about it, and then plan a discussion for the following day. You can always end with, "Let's talk about this again tomorrow."

Do not "analyze" your child's deeper motives.

Do not try and help them understand what they are "really" angry or upset about. When children have become very angry about minor disappointments or provocations, you may feel a need to help them develop some insight—to see a connection between their overreaction and other painful feelings (for example, their jealousy of their siblings or their unhappiness at school). On rare occasions, when they are unusually receptive, you may be successful in this effort and help them gain some increment of self-understanding and emotional maturity.

There are at least two reasons, however, to be cautious about talking with children about their deeper feelings and motives. First, children almost always resent this analysis, which is implicitly dismissive of their conscious concerns. And, to be honest, we are often wrong.

How Can We Promote Our Children's Social and Moral Development?

Acknowledge and value their feelings.

Then teach them about the feelings of others. Listen patiently to their disappointments and frustrations. Be an "emotion coach." In an important series of studies by psychologist John Gottman and his colleagues, children of parents who valued, accepted, and expressed emotions showed better academic achievement, had lower levels of stress hormones, and were more successful in resolving conflicts with their peers.[13]

Speak respectfully—to your children and to each other.

When you talk with your children, speak to them calmly, and speak respectfully to each other. If you are frequently angry and critical, your children will not be well behaved, no matter how much discipline you provide.

Parents are often advised, especially by advocates of firm discipline, to "be the parent." In the long run, I believe a better motto is, "be the grownup." At the end of the day, we can only earn, not demand, our children's respect.

You may, of course, insist that they speak to you respectfully. You can then let them know—and they will more often listen—when their behavior is "over the line." Children who are impulsive and strong willed will require more patience *and* more firmness, more opportunities to practice self-restraint, more frequent praise for every increment of effort and helpfulness, and more moments of repair.

Resolve your conflicts—with your children and with each other.

Your children look up to you. They expect you to behave well, toward them and toward each other. Prolonged conflict between parents is a well-established risk factor for emotional and behavioral problems in children and adolescents.[14]

In their research on marital conflict and children's adjustment, psychologists E. Mark Cummings and Patrick Davies found that children do not "get used to" marital conflict. Instead, they become sensitized—insecure, hypervigilant, and less able to regulate their emotions.

Cummings and Davies emphasize this especially important research finding: Children react to *unresolved* marital conflict with increased emotional distress—anger, preoccupation, and aggression. However, children exposed to marital conflict that is *resolved* show little or no distress.

The good news is this: Children are responsive to even subtle indications that conflict has been resolved, for example, hearing laughter from behind closed doors.[15]

Of course, you will not be able to resolve all of your conflicts. When parents separate or divorce, it is important to demonstrate to children that, even then, at least some collaboration is possible and some conflicts can be solved. Child and family therapists almost universally agree: Expressions of denigration and contempt by parents toward each other are especially harmful to children.

Rules 1, 2, and 3 of buffering children from the traumatic effects of divorce are these: Do not denigrate your child's other parent; help children maintain a close and supportive relationship with both parents; and demonstrate to children that at least some conflicts can be resolved.

Acknowledge your mistakes.

Many of my colleagues believe that "giving in" too frequently is the cause of our children's insistent and unreasonable demands. I disagree. The more frequent problem is not our indulgence or our inconsistency. It is our stubbornness. Too many parents, convinced of their "rightness," refuse to acknowledge their errors and listen with openness to their child's grievance or concerns.

When parents are stubborn and inflexible, children, in turn, become stubborn (and, often, uncommunicative).

When we acknowledge our mistakes; when we let our children know that we have disappointed or embarrassed them; or have spoken to them harshly, or spoken harshly to each other—and when we tell them that we are sorry—we do not lose authority with our children. We gain authority, because our authority is ultimately based on respect.

Include doing for others as a regular part of family life.

Help others. Do community service projects together. Doing good for others is good for others, good for us, and good for our children.

Talk with them, at family dinners, about people you (and they) admire.

Let them know that there is so much good work to be done in the world. Find out who they admire and why they admire them. Help them appreciate what others do for us. Talk with them about the people who build our cities, protect our safety, and save our lives.

Let them know about the good work that they will be able to do, and can do, even now. Help them find projects that will teach them the good feeling of helping others. Helping younger children (and older adults) strengthens children's idealism *and* their self-esteem.

Continue your own lifelong effort at learning.

Let them know that learning does not end after formal education. When you show your children that you value learning, and that you continue to be open to learning, they will also be more open to learning—and to learning from their mistakes.

PART II

Solving Common Problems of Family Life

Chapter 8

Getting Unstuck

Five Essential Steps for Solving Family Problems

The principles of emotional development I have discussed in previous chapters help create a foundation of optimism, resilience, and concern for others in the lives of our children. But we cannot always be positive; we cannot always be as available or as supportive as our children would like us to be; and we will not be able to repair every moment of anger and defiance.

In every family, there will be problems. No matter how positive and empathic we have been, kids will still argue and misbehave, and ask for more than they can have. The stress and demands of our daily lives—and of theirs—will inevitably create conflict and misunderstanding.

Often, there is a recurring problem. The problem may be getting ready for school in the morning or going to sleep at night. Or doing homework, or fighting with siblings. They may be demanding or disrespectful, or refuse to cooperate when asked. Over time, these common problems of daily living begin to erode the quality of our relationships with our children—and our own pleasure in being parents.

Children want to solve problems, and they want to do well. Like us, however, they may become frustrated and even feel hopeless that solutions are possible. Like us, they may become stubborn, defensive, and blaming of others. And, like us, they may just not know what to do.

In the following chapters, I will present specific plans for solving many family problems—a plan for doing homework, for going to sleep, for lack of cooperation, and for children's addiction to television and video games. In this chapter, I will begin with some basic guidelines—essential steps to keep in mind for solving the most common, yet challenging, problems of daily family life.

First, however, a warning: The solution to any common problem of childhood should not be attempted piecemeal. Every anxiety and every problematic behavior our children present to us requires an effort to understand its possible causes. We should not assume that we know *why* a child refuses to do his homework, or does not help with basic chores, or seems addicted to television and video games, or is unable to fall asleep at night.[1]

I will repeat the following advice in a subsequent chapter, but it is important enough to warrant repetition: *Every* child whose parents or teachers observe ongoing resistance to completing schoolwork or homework; *every* child whose performance in school is below expectations based on his parents' or teachers' intuitive assessment of his intellectual potential; and *every* child who, over an extended period of time, complains that he "hates school" or "hates reading" should be evaluated for the presence of an attention or learning disorder—*even when other plausible reasons for a child's academic difficulties (for example, marital conflict, divorce, or medical illness) are also present.*

These children are not "lazy." Your child may be frustrated, discouraged, anxious, distracted, or angry—but this is not laziness.[2]

Step 1: Take a Step Back

The first step in solving any recurring problem in the life of a child is to take a step back. These problems of family life are best solved—and perhaps can *only* be solved—proactively. When we are *reacting* to our children's behavior, we will often be reacting badly. Clinicians and parent advisors of all points of view agree on this point.

Solving children's behavior problems is a little bit like playing tennis or golf. If you're not hitting the ball well, check your grip or your stance before you decide to change your swing. We need to ask ourselves, have I been spending time engaging my child's interests? Have I been, unwittingly, too angry and critical? If he is speaking to me disrespectfully, how have I been speaking to him?

Problems of family life are best solved proactively. When we are *reacting* to our children's behavior, we will often be reacting badly.

A New Understanding of Your Child's Behavior

To solve any problem of family life, we need a plan. Our plan may end with new rules and new consequences for violations of these rules. But it does not begin there.

The solution of every common problem of childhood begins with listening, even if all that your child can tell you is, "I don't know." Always try to begin—whether the problem is frequent tantrums, refusal to do homework, or spending too much time playing video games—with an effort to understand the problem from your child's point of view.

Look for causes, not just symptoms. You will solve these problems more successfully when you have developed a deeper appreciation of the anxiety, frustration, or discouragement that underlies your child's problematic behavior. You need to identify the daily experiences in the life of your child that are sources of painful feelings. These may be frustration in learning, or frequent criticism, or bullying or exclusion. Again, listen to your child's grievance. Let him tell you what he believes is unfair in his life, and *tell him what is right about what he is saying before you tell him what is wrong*. You can say, for example, "I know you feel that we are always on your case about your schoolwork, and maybe we are. But we're worried and we need to solve this problem."

Look for causes, not just symptoms.

Some parents (and parent advisors) chafe at this advice, which feels to them like coddling, too "democratic," or even "namby-pamby." But it is still the right advice. There is plenty of time for rules and consequences.

Every problem of daily living will also be resolved more quickly and more easily when you are able to put into practice basic principles of emotional health and resilience—encouragement and support for your child's interests and projects; frequent, enthusiastic play; and repair of angry and critical interactions. A family atmosphere of frequent criticism and argument undermines our best efforts to solve any common problem.

Step 2: Place the Problem Before Your Child

Once you have identified a recurrent problematic situation and made some effort to understand its causes, your next step is to place the problem before your child. Say, for example, "We have a problem in the morning, when it's time to get ready, and I often end up yelling at you," or "I think we have a shower problem," or "A lot of times, we have a problem when I tell you that it is time to turn off the television."

Step 3: Elicit Your Child's Ideas

It seems almost reflexive for many parents, when faced with a child's persistent defiance or lack of cooperation, to attempt to solve this problem by imposing a "consequence" for their child's misbehavior. Although some problems may require this approach, I recommend that you first engage your child in an effort to solve the problem—to elicit your child's ideas.

In this way (as with Julia from the Introduction to this book), you will often be able to engage your child in a search for solutions. She will then be less absorbed in angry and defiant thoughts, less "stuck" in making demands or continuing the argument. She will begin to think, even if just for that moment, less about getting her way and instead about how to solve a problem, how her needs and the needs of others might be reconciled—an important life lesson, for sure.

Once you have placed the problem before your child and asked for her ideas, give her some time. You can say, for example, "Why don't you think about it for a while? Let's talk again later, or tomorrow, and see what your ideas are." In doing this, you will be teaching yet another important lesson, because this is how most problems in life should be solved.

Listening to your child's ideas does not diminish your authority as a parent. As parents, we retain our authority to establish rules and consequences, and there are many situations, especially those that involve safety and the rights of others, when rules are explained but are not negotiable.

Step 4: Develop a Plan

In my experience, almost all children respond positively when I tell a family that "I have a plan" to solve a recurrent problem of family life. They may be skeptical, but they listen with interest. Deep down, they want a plan, as much as we do.

The plan may involve a new structure (for example, a specified time and place for homework) or a system of responsibilities and earning privileges. It may also be necessary to establish new rules and enforce consequences for persistent or egregious violations of these rules. Children understand this—all families have rules. (I will discuss the problem of establishing family rules and limits in greater detail in the following chapter.)

Problem-Solving Plans: Fundamentals

To begin, here are a few general principles about problem-solving plans.

Every plan includes a delineation of responsibilities—your child's responsibilities and your responsibilities as a parent. Plans should also include a structure—a time and place for talking and expressing worries and concerns, a time when both you and your child will be available to play or to listen—and a time when you will *not* be available. There is a time for discussion and a time when the discussion is over, to be continued later.

Acknowledge your child's frustration and disappointment and then offer some active help in coping with these feelings.

Solving common problems involves some increased ability on the part of your child to anticipate and "handle" disappointment, anxiety, and frustration. Acknowledge your child's frustration or disappointment and then offer some active help in coping with these feelings. Talk about what she can *do* when she is angry or upset—a strategy for regulating her emotions. Or you can offer a new behavior, what behavioral psychologist Alan Kazdin calls a "positive opposite."[3]

Many children, especially if you have expressed an appreciation of their needs and concerns, participate enthusiastically in this process. A child may make a list of "things I can do when I'm upset" (for example, draw, write, or play with her dolls). Or, for a young child who is angry, you can suggest that she go to an "angry spot" or "home base"[4] in her room. Or your child might ask you to use a signal, a word that can be invoked as a warning that her language or behavior is "over the line."

Remember: If you have not first listened to your child's grievance, she will be a half-hearted participant in this problem-solving process, and any strategies you offer are likely to be ineffective.

These techniques are also unlikely to be helpful once a child's distress or anger has passed a certain threshold. Children often tell me that they cannot make use of these techniques, even when they would like to, when they are "too angry." And we have known for a long time that once a tantrum has started, most often it has to run its course.[5]

Step 5: Express Appreciation and Praise for Increments of Effort and Success

Be sure to offer praise and appreciation for every increment of your child's effort at compliance and self-control. Your acknowledgment of her effort and progress is a basic principle of successful problem solving (and of maintaining healthy relationships with our children). This principle has many names. Behavioral scientists call it shaping. In the work of Carol Dweck, it is an aspect of a growth mindset. I like to call it *encouragement and appreciation*.

Often, however, parents neglect this essential step. Children's efforts at cooperation are too quickly taken for granted, or the bar is set too high. Or parents establish a system of earning rewards but fail to follow through. Then, following some initial improvement, a family will tell me that the plan did not work and that they are back to square one.

Psychologists have learned from psychotherapy research that ongoing collaboration is an important element of successful therapy. This is also true in solving problems with our children. We should regularly, proactively, check in with children, and ask, for example, "How do you think we are doing with our morning problem?"

Chapter 9

The Problem of Discipline

How to Set Limits and What Limits to Set

The problem of discipline is an important concern of every parent. For many parents, it has become an overriding concern. How can we gain our children's cooperation and compliance with basic tasks? How can we establish and maintain their respect for our authority? What should we do when our children misbehave?

In short, how we should "discipline" our children?

So much has been written about this problem. Many programs have been presented, many claims and promises have been made. One popular program promises "a new kid by Friday" if parents politely, but firmly, walk away from their children's unreasonable demands.[1]

As always, among child-rearing advisors, opinions about this problem tend to fall into two opposing camps. Advocates of firm discipline tell us that our children speak to us disrespectfully because we allow them to, that we are afraid to insist on obedience and respect. The disciplinarians believe that modern parents are overly solicitous and overly concerned to "soothe each minor unpleasant feeling"; that we have turned our homes into "little democracies" in which children "determine their own upbringing" and have the right to argue about everything.[2]

As a group, these advisors concur: Parents should be less afraid to say, "No."

For some families, this is sound advice. In my experience, for most families, it is not. And this is surely a simplistic (and often convenient) understanding of the problem. In most cases, a child's refusal to cooperate has other causes. In many families, parents continually punish and give children time-outs, but children remain disobedient and disrespectful. These families are stuck in escalating cycles of punishment and defiance that will not be resolved by more firmly saying, "No."

Behavioral scientists who have studied oppositional behavior in children have made significant progress in understanding the origins of—and cure for—these problems. Highly effective programs to reduce defiant behavior in children and early adolescents have been developed and tested. These advances in behavioral techniques now offer proven alternatives to frequent criticism and punishment. It could be said, with only modest exaggeration, that in theory behavioral science has solved the problem of children's oppositional and defiant behavior. It has not been solved by ideological argument but by careful study.[3]

In real life, of course, discipline is difficult. Decisions about how to respond to children's challenging behavior always involve listening and judgment, and some effort to balance empathy and firmness, complicated by our fatigue and our frustration, our anger and impatience.

It is important to keep in mind, especially when parents frequently disagree, that each single decision about a child's behavior is not critical. In any difficult moment, when you need to decide, "Does this misbehavior merit a punishment, or is it better to let this one go?" there may not be a "correct" answer.

Our ultimate goal is to help children develop self-discipline, or discipline in the best sense—the ability to forgo immediate pleasure and to endure disappointment and frustration in the service of long-term goals. *Discipline* is also a noun before it is a verb.

The Solution

The solution to the problem of defiant behavior begins with the basic principles of emotional health and resilience discussed in previous chapters: Be positive. Be proactive. Let them know you are proud of them—for their effort and for their accomplishments. Play with them often. Repair angry and critical interactions.

When there is a problem, engage your child in problem solving. Place the problem before your child and ask for her ideas. Acknowledge her concerns. Let her know your concerns. Be creative—and encourage your child to be creative—in developing strategies for expressing her feelings in constructive, rather than hurtful or destructive, ways. Then, establish rules. When necessary, institute a system of earning privileges for cooperation and consequences for violations of rules.

Discipline, however, should be a small part of family life. We want more for, and from, our children than obedience and respect. We want them to become caring and purposeful adults.

The simplicity of family rules is important. Simple rules are unarguable (most of the time) and more easily enforced.

When we have been able to create a more positive family atmosphere—an atmosphere in which children look forward to spending time with us and are willing to share their concerns (at least some of the time)—the problem of setting limits will be far easier (although, admittedly, especially for impulsive or hyperactive children, it is often far from easy).

In families where there is little positive engagement and supportive listening, and when we are unable to resolve our own conflicts, our attempts to set limits are likely to be difficult—and often unsuccessful. As Alan Kazdin points out, the effectiveness of our time-outs depends largely on the quality of our time-ins.[4]

Rules and Limits

All families have rules. All children know this. The rules are explained to them—and, when necessary, posted on the refrigerator—from an early age. They are taught the same rules in school, at every activity, and at summer camp.

Almost all nonnegotiable family rules fall into three basic categories. We establish rules for the following reasons:

- *To protect our children's health and safety* (for example, children must always wear a seatbelt, or a helmet when riding a bicycle).
- *To respect the rights of others* (for example, a child's language may not be hurtful or abusive, and his brother or sister must also get a turn).
- *To promote values that are particularly important to a given family* (for example, restrictions on watching television or playing violent video games, or attendance at religious observances).

These restrictions on a child's freedom are easily understood—and readily accepted—by most children. I recommend these guidelines for parents who are uncertain about what battles to choose—what rules to strictly enforce and when to allow a child greater choice and freedom of expression.

All children are taught limits on physical and verbal aggression. Younger children are told: No hitting, no screaming, no bad words, and cooperate with parents, especially during recurring problematic moments, for example, getting ready in the morning or going to bed on time. The same rules, of course, apply to older children, with perhaps some others, for example, limits on the use of electronic games and helping with household chores. The simplicity of family rules is important. Simple rules are unarguable (most of the time) and therefore more easily enforced.

In talking with children, I have found it helpful to emphasize the obviousness of a family's need for rules. I may say to young children, "Of course, kids need to have a bed time" or "I never heard of a kid who could watch TV *all day*." And although some children may briefly protest, kids get it. (As parents, we should also obey these basic rules, as a matter of course.)

Earning

Family rules and limits allow us to put into practice a basic principle of emotional maturity that most children come to understand: Children *earn* privileges (and things) rather than *demanding* them.

A simple change of tone and grammar—from "if" to "when" or "as soon as"—often makes a dramatic difference in the cooperativeness of young children.

When children obey family rules, they earn privileges, for example, extra time to watch television or an opportunity to stay up late. Many children like to negotiate, or make lists, of the privileges they want to earn. Earned privileges can be special activities with parents, but children are also motivated by the opportunity to make small purchases, for example, cards, Silly Bands, or Webkinz.

Almost all children look forward to the opportunity to earn recognition and praise from their parents and teachers. Most young children respond enthusiastically to simple reward systems—opportunities to earn stars or stickers, exchanged for privileges—at home and at school.

A system of earning also allows you to move more easily from the threat of punishment ("If you don't . . ., then you won't be able to . . . ") to the principle of "when" or "as soon as." This simple change of tone and grammar—from "if" to "when" or "as soon as"—often makes a dramatic difference in the cooperativeness of young children.[5]

When you establish a system of earning, you should always be willing to listen to what your children want. Then let them know what is possible. With some exceptions (for example, special events that a child learns of at the last minute) negotiations about privileges should take place in advance. Children (especially children who are practiced negotiators) should know that they cannot negotiate all the time, especially when we have already said, "No."

Consequences

So much unnecessary conflict and so much damage to our relationships with our children has been caused by our preoccupation with "consequences." This is especially true when consequences have become the centerpiece of parents' efforts to establish obedience and good behavior.

Again, it seems almost instinctive for many parents to respond to their child's problematic behavior by imposing (or threatening) a consequence. Then, when the consequences are not effective, they believe (incorrectly) that they have not punished their child enough or made the consequences of his misbehavior sufficiently severe.

Let me be clear. I am not endorsing permissiveness, and I am not "against" consequences. Our behavior has consequences. All games and sports have rules—and consequences for violations of rules—and all children know this. Recognizing the consequences of our behavior, and learning from them, is another hallmark of emotional maturity.

When we are frequently threatening "consequences" as the solution to our children's behavior problems, we are doing something wrong.

But when we are frequently threatening consequences for children's noncompliance, or when we are thinking often about consequences as the solution to our children's behavior problems, we are doing something wrong. Our relationships with our children and their emotional health will suffer—and our consequences are unlikely to be effective.[6]

Over the Line

Managing a child's defiant behavior requires patience and is difficult for all parents. When you establish rules and consequences, you should therefore keep them simple: Your child loses a privilege for a relatively brief period of time (for example, you can take away an evening of "screen time").

There are many analogies, especially from sports, that children almost universally understand. I remind both parents and children that a baseball player is allowed (with some restrictions) to argue with an umpire. If he uses profanity, however, or if he continues to argue after the umpire has given him a warning, he is out of the game. (And a player who touches an umpire during an argument is automatically suspended for three games.) Every sport has a similar system of rules—and penalties for infractions—that are well known to children. Soccer offers an especially helpful system. For most first violations, a player receives a warning—a yellow card; if his infraction is especially egregious, he receives a red card and he is out of the game. It is the same with children. When they misbehave, give them a warning—a yellow card—and a chance to start over. Children also know (at least until defiant attitudes have become habitual) when their behavior is over the line.

Here is an essential point: Children understand these rules and *almost always make some initial effort to comply*. If you fail to recognize your child's efforts at compliance, or if you consider them half-hearted or "not enough," your attempts to improve his behavior will fail. Acknowledge his *effort* as well as his successes. You can say, for example, "I could see that you tried really hard to control your temper"—even when he eventually loses his temper.

When you understand this fundamental principle, you will find many more opportunities to express appreciation and praise. I also recommend that parents offer generous "bonuses" to children (or, at least, generous expressions of appreciation) for unsolicited prosocial behavior, for example, helping a younger child feel better.[7]

In my experience, when these simple behavioral systems don't work, other family problems have interfered. Parents may consider the plan onerous and therefore fail to follow through. Or parents find it difficult to express frequent appreciation and praise; they are unable to agree; or an atmosphere of criticism continues unabated. Or parents continue to believe that frequent punishment is a necessary and effective means of teaching compliant behavior. It isn't.

Thomas Phelan has presented a popular technique for managing moments of noncompliance that allows parents to respond to their children's defiant behavior in a calm but still authoritative manner, without yelling and with less arguing. He calls this,

"1-2-3 Magic." Phelan is right. This method, if not magic, is remarkably effective and helpful to many beleaguered parents, especially in responding to fighting among siblings or when children repeatedly ignore their parents' requests. At these moments, parents simply say, "If you don't stop fighting by the time I count to three, you will not be able to (watch a favorite television program or play a video game)." If used in appropriate contexts, children quickly respond and parents rarely reach the count of three.[8]

Why Do Children Misbehave?

Children misbehave because, in the first place, they are being kids. They are exuberant and impulsive—jumping, playing, and not sitting still when we want them to sit quietly. They want to play when the time for play is over, and they don't want to stop when they are having fun. Or they may be angry and envious, and want more than they can have. Or they are making a protest or a demand. They will protest because they want more time to play; they will protest when they are anxious; and they will protest, loudly and vehemently, when they believe that our rules and restrictions are unfair.

At times, children misbehave because we make unreasonable demands. We expect them to sit still and attend, or to entertain themselves and get along together, longer than children can reasonably be expected to do.

Children do not misbehave because they are trying to "make us angry" or "push our buttons"; or because they are inherently sinful; and only occasionally because they are "looking for attention."

Parents often ask, "Why does he keep acting this way? Is he just trying to get attention?" The answer, again, is, "He is caught up in the emotion (and need) of the moment," whether the emotion of the moment is an angry or anxious feeling, a need to feel accepted, a need to win, or a need to undo a feeling of embarrassment or loneliness.

Very often, a child's difficult behavior begins with a difficult temperament. Tantrums and uncooperative behavior are far more frequent among children who are, in their basic temperament, anxious, inattentive, impulsive, or strong willed. Over time, our reactions to their misbehavior, especially when we are frequently angry and critical, set in motion vicious cycles of "coercive" family interactions.[9]

In the course of these battles, both we and our children become increasingly angry and inflexible. Coercive interactions are profoundly destructive—destructive of a child's initiative and his sense of responsibility—and an established risk factor for antisocial behavior. The first and most important step in solving children's behavior problems is to arrest this malignant development.

Alan Kazdin and his colleagues at the Yale Child Study Center have developed a behavioral program that reports close to an 80% success rate with children who present severe behavior problems. This program, developed and tested for children with severe oppositional and defiant behavior, is good for all children. In my work with families of impulsive, strong-willed, or defiant children, I recommend the Kazdin Method as the state of the art in helping change children's oppositional behavior.

Effective programs to reduce defiant behavior in children and adolescents, like the Kazdin Method, are now based on the principle of *positive* reinforcement. Parents of defiant children are advised to be more positive, in all ways, with their children. We need to focus our attention less (or not at all) on what we want our children *not* to do, but instead on what we want them *to* do, what Kazdin calls a "positive opposite." We need to teach and reward positive alternatives to misbehavior. Praise—generous and enthusiastic praise—has taken precedence over punishment or consequences in contemporary behavior management programs.

Psychologist Alan Kazdin wisely advises parents to "praise little steps, good tries, and almost-behaviors" even when they fall short of the desired goal.

Kazdin's research reaffirms the classic child-rearing wisdom, to "catch your child being good." He wisely advises that "it's critical to praise little steps, good tries, and almost-behaviors" even when they fall short of the desired goal. And he correctly adds, "Don't be stingy about this."[10]

When I began my clinical practice (and still today), I could not have been a behaviorist. The language of behaviorism—reinforcement, conditioning, shaping, extinction—was (and is) alien to my way of thinking about children. Behaviorist principles left out what was (and is), for me, most essential and most meaningful about being a parent, and early behaviorist programs for children extended these principles and techniques far beyond the range of problems for which they might be applicable.

Behaviorism, however, has matured. Contemporary behavior therapy programs have become both more effective and also more modest. Behavior management no longer represents a "philosophy" of parenting, and the techniques of behaviorism are no longer considered the solution to all family problems.[11] A program of earning privileges can be remarkably helpful in our effort to arrest malignant cycles of family interactions and restore positiveness in the lives of children and parents.

Chapter 10

Homework

Battles over homework, in my experience, are the most common source of conflict between parents and children in middle-class, suburban families. I have half-jokingly told many parents that if the schools of New York State no longer required homework, our children's education would suffer (slightly), but, as a child psychologist, I would be out of business.

Many parents accept this conflict with their children as yet another unavoidable consequence of responsible parenting. These battles, however, rarely result in improved learning or performance in school. More often than not, battles over homework lead to vicious cycles of nagging by parents and avoidance or refusal by children, with no improvement in a child's school performance—and certainly no progress toward what should be our ultimate goals: helping children enjoy learning and develop age-appropriate discipline and independence with respect to their schoolwork.

The solution to the problem of homework *always* begins with an accurate diagnosis and a recognition of the demands placed on your child. You should *never* assume that a child who resists doing homework is "lazy."

Every child whose parents or teachers report ongoing resistance to completing schoolwork or homework; *every* child whose performance in school is below expectations based on his parents' or teachers' intuitive assessment of his intellectual potential; and *every* child who, over an extended period of time, complains that he "hates school" or "hates reading" should be evaluated for the presence of an attention or learning disorder. These evaluations are essential even when there are other plausible reasons for a child's academic difficulties, for example, marital conflict, divorce, or medical illness.

These children are not "lazy." Your child may be anxious, frustrated, discouraged, distracted, or angry—but this is not laziness.[1]

A diagnosis of laziness, however, is still unfortunately common. I frequently explain to parents that, as a psychologist, the word *lazy* (and, especially, "just lazy") is not in my dictionary. "Lazy," at best, is a description, not an explanation.

When we believe that a child is lazy, we are left with only one prescription: He must "try harder." This incorrect understanding then leads, almost inexorably, to conflict and stubbornness, and then to increasing demoralization and defiant moods.

For children with learning difficulties, doing homework is like running with a sprained ankle: It is possible but painful.

For children with learning difficulties of all kinds, doing their homework is like running with a sprained ankle: It is possible, although painful, and he will look for ways to avoid or postpone this painful and discouraging task. Or he may run ten steps and then find a reason to stop.

Often his effort is inconsistent. He will put forth effort one day, but not the next. His inconsistent effort is a source of puzzlement and confusion to his parents and teachers. His teachers may believe that "he can do it when he tries" and there is some truth in this observation.

Still, this is an unfortunate misunderstanding. No one can run with a broken ankle. Most attention and learning problems, however, are more like sprains than fractures. On some occasions, when a child's intrinsic interest, or anticipated success, or our encouragement, or the promise of a material reward, is great enough, he will overcome his frustration and put good effort into the task. But he cannot do this every day. I might run a mile with a sprained ankle for the chance to play a round of golf with Tom Watson or Tiger Woods, but I would not do this the day before or the day after.[2]

Children with learning disabilities *always* experience frequent moments of frustration and discouragement. Many suffer chronic feelings of shame and low self-esteem, often masked by defensive or defiant attitudes. As adolescents, these children may continue to feel that they are "not smart," despite considerable talents, areas of academic competence, and interpersonal skills that will serve them well in life.

Recently, in talking with children and adolescents I have evaluated for possible learning disabilities, or children I am working with in psychotherapy, I have made literal use of the idea of our "self-image." I tell the child (and explain to her parents) that I am going to draw a picture of her. I then draw a blank rectangle. In the center of the rectangle, I place the child's strengths—her friendships; her athletic, or musical, or artistic, or dramatic talents; her reasoning and problem-solving abilities. In the corner of the picture, I draw her difficulties—perhaps a problem with math or writing, or that, right now, she needs some help in reading. This exercise may seem simplistic, even a little contrived. Often, however, this is not how children (or their parents) have come to see themselves. Children need to be helped to change this picture, their self-image, to one in which their strengths are in the center and their difficulties are in the corner, not, as is so often the case, the other way around.

We also need to take a step back and reconsider the problem of a child's "motivation." What enables any child to put forth sustained effort on difficult or frustrating tasks—and this is true for all of us, children no less than adults—is the anticipation of future success. Fear of consequences (for example, a bad grade or the disapproval of parents and teachers) may motivate some children to complete their work in the short term, but it cannot sustain a child's motivation and effort in the long run. Her effort eventually fades. Increasingly, she is willing to risk disapproval (or trade certain disapproval) for the short-term relief of anxiety and frustration. She then hides her anxiety with a façade of indifference or "not caring."

Many children who struggle with homework have difficulty getting started. The assigned task, whether because of the demand for sustained attention or, often, for written output, seems overwhelming, as if we were asked to read *War and Peace* in one evening and report on it the following day. Her refusal or procrastination is an expression of frustration and discouragement, and then protest.

A Homework Plan

Homework, like any constructive activity, involves moments of discouragement, frustration, and anxiety. Children who have developed a greater capacity to tolerate anxiety and frustration—children who believe that this work, however onerous, is temporary and therefore bearable and, especially, children who believe that their work will result in some success (and recognition of their success)—will more effectively cope with this (or any) difficult task.

Like many other unpleasant tasks, homework has to be done. If you begin with some understanding of your child's frustration and discouragement, you will be better able to put in place a structure that helps him learn to work through his frustration—to develop increments of frustration tolerance and self-discipline.

I offer families who struggle with this problem a Homework Plan:

- Set aside a specified—and limited—time for homework. Establish, early in the evening, a homework hour.
- For most children, immediately after school is not the best time for homework. This is a time for sports, for music and drama, and free play.
- During the homework hour, all electronics are turned off—for the entire family.
- Work is done in a communal place, at the kitchen or dining room table. Contrary to older conventional wisdom, most elementary school children are able to work much more effectively in a common area, with an adult and even other children present, than in the "quiet" of their rooms.
- Parents may do their own "homework" during this time, but they are present and continually available to help, to offer encouragement, and to answer children's questions. Your goal is to create, to the extent possible, a library atmosphere in your home, again, for a specified and limited period of time. Ideally, therefore, parents should not make or receive telephone calls during this hour. And when homework is done, there is time for play.
- Begin with a reasonable—a doable—amount of time set aside for homework. If your child is unable to work for 20 minutes, begin with 10 minutes. Then try 15 minutes the next week. Acknowledge every increment of effort, however small.
- Anticipate setbacks. After a difficult day, reset for the following day.
- Give them time. A child's difficulty completing homework begins as a problem of frustration and discouragement, but it is then complicated by defiant attitudes and feelings of

unfairness. A homework plan will begin to reduce these defiant attitudes, but this will not happen overnight.

Most families have found these suggestions helpful, especially for elementary school children.[3] Establishing a homework hour allows parents to move, again, away from a language of *threats* ("If you don't . . . you won't be able to . . .") to a language of *opportunities* ("When" or "As soon as" you have finished . . . we'll have a chance to . . .").

Of course, for many hurried families, there are complications and potential glitches in implementing any homework plan. It is often difficult, with children's many activities, to find a consistent time for homework. Some flexibility—some amendments to the plan—may be required. But we should not use the complications of scheduling or other competing demands as an excuse, a reason not to establish the structure of a reasonable homework routine.

Too Much Homework or Too Little?

The homework debate continues.

Social critics, alarmed by an apparent decline in our nation's educational standards and our global competitiveness, believe that schools need to expect more of our students, including more homework. Many parents and educators, however, are equally alarmed—by evidence of increased anxiety and stress in students of all ages. I share these concerns. In the communities where I live and work, the increasing academic demands placed on students, early in childhood, have often done more harm than good, causing unnecessary conflict between parents and children, and eroding students' enjoyment of learning.

Again, social science offers us some guidance. Duke University psychologist Harris Cooper, based on a comprehensive review of research, recommends that school districts adopt a "10-minute rule"—students and parents "should expect all homework assignments together to last as long as 10 minutes multiplied by the student's grade level" (or perhaps 15 minutes if required reading time is included). Cooper believes that beyond 15 minutes per grade, "the costs of homework will begin to outweigh the benefits."[4] Cooper's recommendations have been accepted by the National Parent-Teacher Association.

The answer to the question of whether your child is doing too much homework would seem to depend on where you live. In some communities, the amount of time students are expected to spend doing homework far exceeds these research-based recommendations. National surveys, however, present a different picture. Across the country, homework has not increased since the 1980s and most high school students spend less than 1 hour a night on homework.[5]

Over a decade ago, Piscataway, New Jersey, because of concerns that homework demands were having a destructive effect on family life, limited the amount of homework teachers could assign—to a maximum of 30 minutes per day for elementary school students and 2 hours for high school students. The long-term success of this (in my opinion, very reasonable) experiment, of course, is unknown and difficult to evaluate. Media reports at the time, however, indicated that the Piscataway plan was greeted approvingly by a large majority of parents in the community.

Chapter 11

"Why Won't She Talk to Us?"

"How was school today?"
"Good."
"What did you do?"
"Stuff."

It is disheartening, but true: Children often do not want to talk to us, or anyone, about their bad feelings. And not only about bad feelings. Parents often express concern about their child's general uncommunicativeness—her frequent defensiveness and unwillingness to engage in any dialogue, even to report mundane events of the day.

As child therapists, many parents consult us with the (not unreasonable) hope that this is our special skill—that we will be able to help their child "open up," tell them what is wrong, and talk with them. In a sense, of course, these parents are right: There is an art to child therapy and we continually strive to perfect this art—to find, for each child, some unique blend of empathy and patience, playfulness and humor, that will help a child learn that talking about bad feelings *does* help, at least some of the time.

There is an art, but there is no magic. Children tell even their most warm and accepting therapists, in response to our most tactful inquiries about their evident emotional distress or about the events of past days and weeks, "I don't remember" or "I don't know." Even more strenuously, children do not want *us* to talk to *them*. Experienced child therapists, masters of their craft, routinely report that "as usual, my words had little impact."[1]

Our children's reluctance to talk with us remains our persistent nemesis. Children hide their bad feelings. They do not let us in, and they make it difficult for us to convey our empathy, at least not in a straightforward way.

What Can We Do?

We begin, as always, with our genuine interest in our child's interests. This advice is important enough to say again: *As parents, our enthusiastic interest in our children's interests is the surest way to engage a child in some form of meaningful dialogue or interaction.*

Nothing helps children more than knowing that we, their parents, have also suffered disappointment and defeat, rejection and exclusion—and that we have bounced back.

We then add to this our empathic recognition of a child's distress or grievance. In my work as a child therapist, I have learned a second principle of talking with children: When a child is sullen and uncommunicative, if I ask her to tell me about what is unfair in her life, she will almost always open up.

These basic attitudes—enthusiastic interest in our children's interests and acknowledgment of a child's grievance—allow almost all children to engage with us in some dialogue, even if sometimes brief, about a problem in their lives.

But we can do more and want to do more. We want our children to know that talking about bad feelings is a normal and helpful thing to do.

When children are angry, we need to acknowledge their protest or their defiant mood. We need to convey, in words and in actions, that we appreciate what is important to them. We need to be playful and make use of humor. And it is often helpful for us to talk about ourselves, about our own frustrations and disappointments.

Nothing helps children more than knowing that we all have bad feelings—that we, their parents, have also suffered disappointment and defeat, rejection and exclusion, even some form of bullying, and that we have bounced back. In therapy, I talk with children about how "a lot of times, kids feel bad when . . . " —that these are feelings all kids have. When we speak in this way, we help our children feel less alone, less ashamed, and less guilty.

We All Have Bad Feelings

Why don't children want to talk with us about their bad feelings? Why do they so often tell us, when we clearly know otherwise, that "everything is fine"? Why do young children put their fingers in their ears, or shout over us, ignore our questions, or say to us, "I'm not going to tell you." Why do they so often refuse to listen to what we have to say? And what can we do about this?

It may be helpful, in thinking about these problems, to keep in mind that children are not alone in their reluctance to acknowledge and talk about bad feelings. Your child's reluctance to talk (what we call her "resistance") is sometimes less subtle than our own. But we all do this, to some degree. We hide our anxiety, our insecurity, and our self-doubt behind a multitude of avoidances and "reasons," and we may stubbornly cling to these attitudes and behaviors, just as our children do. In everyday life, our resistance is expressed in our reluctance to consider new ideas and in our opposition to anything that challenges our sense of security. Resistance is the reason we so often fail to understand ourselves—and each other—and the reason that psychotherapy takes time.

Your child's unwillingness to talk to you is an instinctive self-protective behavior, evoked by her anticipation of painful feelings. Children refuse to talk to us because they are angry or ashamed, or they are afraid that we will be critical, or that talking will not help them feel better. When we ask a child a question, often, he has come to hear more than just the question. He hears the overtones, the implications, of our questions. He knows, intuitively, that many of our "neutral" questions are not really neutral. He may wonder, why are you asking me about *this*?

In my discussions with children of different ages, I have found four common reasons why children do not want to talk.

"Too Much Talk"

In therapy, children often complain about "too much talk." Behind this statement, they are often afraid that talking will just make them feel bad "all over again," and this fear is not without some justification. A child's bad feelings are not always present. For the moment, he may have established a tenuous, but good enough, emotional equilibrium, some relief from feeling bad, and he does not want this equilibrium threatened. If we would just leave him alone, he believes, his bad feelings will go away.

When we present this understanding to children, when we say, for example, "I think sometimes kids are afraid that if they talk about a problem, they're just going to feel bad . . . they don't want to feel bad all over again . . . they think that talking isn't going to help," many children will acknowledge this fear.

And, of course, we should admit, it is sometimes true that "when you talk about bad feelings, sometimes, for a minute, you *do* feel bad again." We can then add our opinion that "It's still good to talk sometimes, because then you can figure out a way to solve a problem, something that helps you feel better."

"There Is Nothing Wrong With Me"

A child's fear that there is "something wrong" with her is perhaps her deepest reason for not talking. (Too often, children have been told that there *is* something wrong with them, for example, when, in exasperation, parents have asked, "What is wrong with you?" or told her that she is "bad.") At these moments, a child's silence is motivated by her need to protect herself from a feeling of shame. This is why most children are more willing to talk about their *worries* than about other bad feelings, because worries do not threaten a child's self-esteem as directly, for example, as a feeling of being rejected by peers.

A child's fear that there is "something wrong" with her is perhaps her deepest reason for not talking.

Children cannot talk about these painful feelings *because they are too painful*. They are afraid of what we might say to them, that we may confirm their unspoken fear—that there *is* something wrong with them—or that we might *blame* them (and they therefore vehemently blame others). When a child begins to sense in our questions, an implication, even a hint, that we think they have a *big* problem, not just *regular* problems that "a lot of kids have," she is likely to quickly become defensive or refuse to talk. When we let children know that a lot of kids feel this way, or have this problem, or, better yet, that *we* have also had this bad feeling, they often visibly relax and, sometime later, open up.

Protest and Argument

Children may also refuse to talk as an act of protest or argument. Recall that every criticism, or anticipation of criticism, evokes some defensiveness in all of us, and that every emotional injury leads to some hardening of a child's protective shell. When we are frequently critical, children will shut down or turn away.

In many families, criticism, argument, and unproductive discussion have become habitual; your child is now chronically defensive, engaged in ongoing inner argument. When you ask her to talk, she anticipates more criticism, or she may just be too angry to talk. In these cases, your child's unwillingness to talk with you is a form of protest—a private vow of silence.

"Talking Doesn't Help"

Many children have developed a sense of futility about talking and a conviction that talking will not help. They may have made some effort to talk with their parents, to explain how they feel, especially, to convey feelings of unfairness. But the conversations have not gone well. Their parents may have taken over the talking and not spent enough time listening. Children then come to believe that "talking" means being "talked to."

There are still other reasons for a child's unwillingness to talk: She may be anxious about your disapproval, or she may need to protect a feeling of autonomy ("I want to do it myself"). Some children don't seem to know how to talk about feelings at all.

How Can We Promote Our Children's Willingness to Talk With Us?

Most of the following recommendations have already been presented in the course of discussing other difficulties in family relationships. The problem of communication with our children, it would seem, is not really a different problem but depends on the quality of our interest, our listening, and our support.

- Hang out with them. Watch a television program together. It is well known that children often open up at unscheduled times.
- Set aside 10 minutes, every evening, as a time to talk—a time to listen to your child's concerns and to share stories. If she says that she has nothing to tell you, tell her about something that happened in your day, perhaps a moment of excitement or frustration, or a moment of humor. Ask her about something she is looking forward to, or worried about, the next day.
- Listen to her grievances, what she feels is unfair in her life. *Acknowledge what is right about what she is saying before you tell her what is wrong.*
- Be personal. Tell personal stories. Tell her about when you were a girl or boy.
- Be playful. Use humor (but not sarcasm). When working with children in therapy, I like to pretend that I am a Jedi knight (or an evil Sith lord) who tries to use the Force to control a child's thoughts and actions; or that I recently bought a "mind reader" from a local store, a new invention that allows me to know what a child is thinking. Almost all children smile at this silliness, and they are delighted that these devices never work—their powers can always

defeat mine. Playfulness and humor are not magic. Our humor is often able to lighten a child's mood, but he will not immediately open up. We have laid the groundwork, however, for another time.

- Be patient. Give them time.
- Be careful how you talk about others. If you are frequently judgmental of others, your children may become anxious that you will also be critical and judgmental of them.
- Repair moments of anger and criticism.
- Acknowledge your mistakes.

There are many other time-honored techniques for facilitating communication with young children. Children are often willing to draw, or write, or speak through puppets and action figures, instead of talk. These techniques often create just enough distance to allow children to express thoughts and feelings they are afraid to say to us directly. But even then, when they write, they may still write, "No talk."

Chapter 12

"He's Not Motivated"

As a child therapist, I am often told, "He's not motivated. All he wants to do is watch television or play video games." Parents urgently ask, "Why doesn't he put more effort into his schoolwork? Why doesn't he care?" Again, I may be told that a child is lazy.

Most often, parents express these concerns about their child's schoolwork. For other children, however, their apparent lack of motivation goes further. These children seem to lack enthusiasm or passion for any activity. Or they are briefly passionate, then run out of steam, or give up easily in everything they do.

The answer to these questions is almost always, "Because he is discouraged." He may also be anxious or angry, and he is stuck in this bad mood. He feels that putting effort into his schoolwork is not "worth it" and it is easier for him to pretend that he doesn't care. He may mask his discouragement with defiance or blame others (especially his teachers) for his lack of effort. He will seek relief in activities that require little sustained effort and that offer, instead, some immediate feeling of success. The problem of "lack of motivation" is the problem of demoralization, whether overt or disguised.

To solve the problem of a child's lack of motivation, we need to return to first principles: Children, when they are not angry or discouraged, want to do well. They want to feel good about themselves—and about others. They want to earn our praise and approval, and they want us to be proud of them. Children say that they don't care, but they do care.

Sustained effort is a different matter. Our ability to work hard, to sustain effort at any task, requires a feeling of accomplishment or progress along the way, and some confidence in our eventual success. All constructive activity involves moments of anxiety, frustration, and discouragement. Children who are "not motivated" too readily give in to these feelings; they do not bounce back.

The problem of "lack of motivation" is the problem of demoralization, whether overt or disguised.

Children often hide their anxiety and discouragement behind defiant and rebellious attitudes. "What is the point of studying history or math anyway, I'm never going to use it." "Who cares who the King of England was in 1850?" Good teachers—teachers who encourage and inspire children, and then demonstrate the relevance of learning—can help us here. But a demoralized child is unlikely to find any relevance in what we want to teach him. He will then be criticized, repeatedly, for his lack of effort, and he will become more rebellious. And he will look elsewhere for a feeling of acceptance and a feeling of pride.

A Personal Example

As I sit down this morning to work on this book, I feel hopeful and energetic. I believe that it will be a good book, helpful to many parents. My colleagues will respect the work that I have done. My parents, although deceased, would be proud of my effort and my success. (It is remarkable. Even at 60 years old, I find that my parents' pride and approval remain meaningful and sustaining.) I have no difficulty "motivating" myself to put in the effort required.

But I did not feel this way yesterday.

Yesterday, I felt anxious and discouraged. I looked at what I had written, and it wasn't very good—old hat, nothing new. I knew what I wanted to say, but I couldn't find the right words to convey my thoughts in a helpful or interesting way. I felt frustrated and began to doubt my ideas. Am I missing something? Is there some important part of children's emotional development that I have overlooked? Is there something not quite right about the recommendations I am now presenting to the public?

The promise of rewards will not help motivate me in these moments. If this is not a good book, there will be no rewards—only wasted time and effort, when I could have been having fun or doing other things. The threat of consequences—a missed deadline—will not help very much either, certainly not in the long run.

It will not help if someone tells me that I should try harder. This will only make me feel angry and misunderstood. I am trying as hard as I can. I may become stubborn and refuse to accept any help. I want to "do it myself," and I don't want my inadequate work to be seen by others. I may sulk or procrastinate. I find myself in a bad mood, resentful of other obligations. As an adult, I am less likely than a child to become stuck in these immature attitudes. But I am certainly not immune from them.

After a while, I am able to bounce back. I recall the encouragement of colleagues and friends who have told me that my ideas are helpful and worthwhile. I remember past moments of discouragement and doubt, and that I found a way to solve those problems. I make a little progress. The chapter is still not as good as I want it to be, but it is a little better than it was yesterday. I think I can make it even better.

It is the same, of course, with children, in everything they do, whether they are writing a book report, solving math problems, playing tennis, or practicing an instrument.

How often do we understand the problem of our children's motivation in this way? How often do we see a child's lack of effort not as a problem of demoralization but as a "behavior" problem? How often do we blame the influence of peers, or television and other media distractions? How often do we become frustrated and angry, and then, in our frustration, tell him that he just has to work harder?

Children are not lazy. They may be frustrated and discouraged, anxious or angry; they may have become disillusioned or defiant, self-critical or pessimistic, and they may lack confidence in their ability. But this is not laziness. The misconception that kids are lazy is one of the most common, and most destructive, misunderstandings of children. It is one of the most important misunderstandings that I (and others) hope to correct.

When you understand your child's lack of motivation as a problem of demoralization, you will be able to look for the real causes of her lack of enthusiasm and effort, and you will be more likely to find helpful solutions.

Undiagnosed (or underappreciated) attention and learning disorders are the most common source of discouragement and lack of sustained effort ("motivation") in children. For these children, doing schoolwork or homework is, again, like running with a sprained ankle—it is possible, although painful. Like all of us, children will find ways to avoid or postpone this painful and discouraging task, and they will look for excuses to cover up their frustration and discouragement.

There are still other reasons for a child's lack of motivation. Children who are "not motivated" are often anxious or angry. They may have been criticized repeatedly for their lack of effort. They now anticipate criticism, instead of encouragement. Their lack of effort has become an act of protest and rebellion.

Persistent criticism is deeply destructive to a child's initiative and confidence. The combination of academic failure and parental scorn can be a lethal mixture for some adolescents.

They may also have become disillusioned. When children no longer look up to us or respect us, if our lives no longer feel to them like the lives they want for themselves, then hard work has lost some of its purpose and meaning.

And, of course, children compare themselves to others. They compare themselves to their parents, their siblings, and their peers. They may feel that they will never be "as good as" others. These feelings are often deeply painful and, again, deeply destructive to a child's motivation and effort.

Motivation begins with interest. Where there is interest, there is curiosity and a desire to know more.

We all want, in some way, to distinguish ourselves. If one child in a family is favored, her siblings may live with a lifelong feeling of resentment and envy. If we compare our children, this will only cause them to feel more resentment and more envy. But even when we do not compare them, they will compare themselves, and compete for our approval.

Finally, some older children and adolescents may not yet have found an interest that feels like their own. They still feel that schoolwork, or athletics, or music is *our* interest, what *we* want for them, not what they want for themselves.

What Really Motivates Children?

Motivation begins with interest. Interest leads to exploration and learning, and to the development of projects. Projects then become ambitions and goals.

Like all of us, children want to do what makes them feel good. They want to do what they are "good at." They want to shine and feel proud. And they want us to be proud of them.

Sustained effort requires confidence in our eventual success. Children are able to sustain motivation and effort when they are confident that they can achieve their goals.

Children need recognition of their effort and their accomplishments. We all do. A child's need for recognition is a deeply intrinsic need, just as intrinsic and just as important as any other.

Children's motivation is also sustained by ideals. Children want to become like, to learn from, and to earn the respect of the people they admire.

Rewards and punishment have some short-term effect on children's effort. We are all motivated, to some extent, to earn rewards and avoid punishment. But rewards and punishment cannot create interests or goals.

I sometimes think of children's motivation in the form of equations:

Motivation = interest + a sense of one's competence + relevance + ideals

Motivation = interest + confidence (the anticipation of success) + the anticipation of recognition (praise or appreciation) for our effort

Motivation = having a goal + feeling that we can achieve it

How Can We Strengthen Our Children's Motivation to Learn and, Eventually, Their Sense of Purpose?

Begin with enthusiastic interest in your child's interests—even if these are not the interests you would choose.

If you look hard enough, you will find in your child some interest—and a desire to do well. When I talk with "unmotivated" students, I often find that they are interested in many things (although not in their schoolwork). They may watch the History or Discovery channels, but they will not read a history or science book. Some read *National Geographic* magazine in my waiting room, but they do not do their homework. Others talk to me about Greek mythology but fall asleep in class. Many are interested in sports, in theater, or in fashion, in *Seinfeld* and *South Park*, in Chris Rock and Jon Stewart, and in theories about the origin of the universe. Often they are interested in music. To my chagrin, few know the music of Dizzy Gillespie or Clifford Brown. But most like music, and they are almost always willing to tell me about it.

Many of these children, to their parents' great dismay, spend hours searching Web sites when they should be studying. Even more have become addicted to video and computer games, to World of Warcraft or Call of Duty. We may disapprove, but these are their interests. And where there is interest, there is curiosity and a desire to learn, to know more.

You need, first, to engage your child's interests, and then to expand these interests into constructive projects and long-term goals. Make note of moments of interest and effort, and support them. If your child is interested in skateboarding, in watching television, or in playing video games, find out why these activities appeal to him. If he likes playing video games, watch him play. Then play with him. Have him teach you the game.

When I ask children about their interests, they are usually happy to talk. I am sure that many of the children and adolescents I see in therapy continue to talk with me for this reason alone—because of my enthusiastic interest in their interests—and this sustains them through the harder work of resolving conflicts. Then, *as long as we are respectful and not dismissive*, they are usually willing, and often eager, to hear our point of view. They *want* to know what we think.

My child and adolescent patients know my opinions about many things. We are now having a conversation about interests and values. If you are dismissive, however, you will lose them.

In these discussions, I often ask children whether they have shared their interests with their parents. Too often, I am told, "My parents don't care about this. They only care about my grades." When I talk with the child's parents, I may learn that this is not, in fact, true. But, in their understandable effort to help their child "improve," they have neglected this vital aspect of children's development and motivation, as my colleagues and I also sometimes do, in our zeal to solve a child's problems.

If we want to motivate our children, to build a bridge, we cannot simply meet them halfway. We must do more than that. In his work with autistic children, child psychiatrist Stanley Greenspan taught both parents and child therapists this seminal insight—that even the repetitive behavior of a 2-year-old child who is rubbing the carpet is an expression of interest, and this interest can become the beginning of an interaction, then play, and then dialogue. If we dismiss our children's interests as frivolous or unproductive, we will miss an opportunity to engage them in dialogue.

William Damon, based on his interviews with purposeful children and young adults, offers this wise advice: "Listen closely for the spark, then fan the flames."[1]

Find the source of their frustration and discouragement.

When children are discouraged, they often say that they *hate* school or *hate* homework. Or that it is "pointless" and irrelevant. We will rarely be able to talk them out of this, no matter how hard we try.

Instead, we need to listen patiently to their frustrations and their grievances. We may even have to listen (more patiently than we would like) to rationalizations and excuses that have only a grain (or less) of truth. Demoralized children are likely to tell us that it's not their fault, that their teachers are unfair. They are discouraged (and inwardly ashamed), but they hide their discouragement.

Again, undiagnosed attention and learning disorders are the most common source of discouragement and lack of sustained effort in children and adolescents. It is essential for both parents and teachers to understand the impact of these difficulties. Even mild or moderate attention and learning problems can be a source of anxiety and frustration for children, leading to discouragement, pessimism, and giving up.

Encouragement, encouragement, encouragement.

Listen for the great sound or the creative idea. Our role model in this should be Dorothy Delay, Itzak Perlman's teacher, whose philosophy and teaching methods I described in Chapter 7.

The solution to a child's lack of motivation is understanding and encouragement, not criticism. There are times in a child's life when criticism is necessary and important. But if the problem is demoralization, criticism will not be helpful.

Acknowledge every increment of effort and progress, and express confidence in your child's eventual success. Make note of his improvement, not his mistakes.

Acknowledge every increment of effort and progress, and express confidence in their eventual success. This may be the essence of encouragement: We make note of a child's improvement and his progress toward goals, not his mistakes.

Acknowledge their frustration, discouragement, and disappointment. Let them know that we understand their feelings, because we have also been frustrated and discouraged.

More than anything else, it may help them to know that we have also had these feelings.

Remind them, when they are ready to hear it, of the good things they have done and will be able to do, and that no one succeeds all the time. Help them put this failure—whether it is a social rejection, an academic disappointment, an athletic defeat, or a disappointment in any area of endeavor—in perspective. There will be a next time.

Tell them, "I know that you are feeling frustrated and disappointed right now, but I have confidence in you. I know that if we put our heads together, we can figure out a way to solve this problem, and you will do better next time."

Recall Coach Carter's philosophy: "If you get one percent better a day, within 100 days you'll be 100 percent better."[2]

Help them develop a different picture of themselves. Their strengths should be in the center of the picture; their difficulties and frustrations should be in the corner.

Remind them of people they admire who have also suffered frustration, disappointment, and defeat. This is the moral of so many of the inspirational stories children read, real stories of Abraham Lincoln and Teddy Roosevelt; Althea Gibson and Jackie Robinson; Sandra Day O'Connor, Ronald Reagan, and Barack Obama.

Talking to children about the importance of effort and hard work, however well intentioned and however true, or grounding them for their avoidance of schoolwork, will not help. Children have heard this all before. Telling them that they have to try harder will only make them feel angry and misunderstood.

Then, engage your child in proactive problem solving.

Give him time.

Don't give up. Solving the problem of motivation will take time. Demoralization has developed over time. It will take time for your child to learn to overcome his pessimism and self-doubt and to let go of cynical and defiant attitudes. Over time, he has become sensitized to disappointments and stuck in moments of frustration. The more that his demoralization has spread, the more that his pessimism and rebellion have become habitual, the more time he will need.

Find a project, for your child and as a family, that involves helping others.

Research on children's involvement in community service (for example, tutoring younger children) has demonstrated the great value of these activities. Children learn from experiences of helping others that they have something to offer—and that helping others feels good. As a side benefit, they also begin to appreciate our perspective as parents, when, for example, they are struggling to get younger children to listen and pay attention.

Chapter 13

Tantrums and Meltdowns

The traditional, and still conventional, wisdom about children's tantrums is this: Tantrums are "manipulative." The cure is not to give in. Stay firm. Don't reward a child's tantrum. Don't be afraid to say, "No." Don't let them wear you down.

This is sound advice. But it is not the whole story.

Tantrums, at any age, are expressions of protest. All young children protest—they cry or even hit—when they are frustrated and disappointed. The extent to which a child is able to respond to common frustrations and disappointments *without* having a tantrum—to be reasonable in his demands—may serve as a rough measure of his emotional maturity. (And our ability, as parents, to respond to a child's tantrum without "having a tantrum back" may be a measure of *our* emotional maturity.)

In the moment of a tantrum, a child's emotions remain urgent ("I have to have this *now*") and inflexible ("No, I have to have *that* one"). His thinking is likely to be all or nothing and pessimistic ("I *never* get what I want"). He feels a sense of grievance and unfairness.

Over time, tantrums may also become manipulative. A child may learn that his tantrums "work"—that if he protests loudly and long enough, we will eventually give in. Some children are willing to acknowledge this. They tell us openly, "My parents threaten to punish me, but they never do." And there may be an element of manipulation in most tantrums; children are, after all, trying to get their way.

But the real problem is that he has not learned to handle frustration and disappointment. Why is he having a meltdown? Because he is angry, he is anxious, or he is frustrated, and he is caught up in the emotion of the moment. His need feels urgent. He cannot wait. He cannot bear the feeling of losing a game. His feelings have been hurt and he must get revenge. Especially when he is angry and lashing out, the threat of punishment or consequences for his actions is unlikely to help. Often, he has made a calculation that, at least for now, the consequences of his behavior don't matter.

The cure for frequent tantrums is to strengthen your child's emotion-regulation and problem-solving skills.

Children who have frequent tantrums are stuck in a *demand* mode, rather than a *problem-solving* mode, of coping with emotional distress. The cure for frequent tantrums and meltdowns is therefore to strengthen a child's emotion-regulation and problem-solving skills. We solve the problem of tantrums when we are able to help children move away from *now*—away from urgent and immediate demands—and toward tolerance for frustration and delay.

What Can We Do?

The problem of frequent tantrums can only be solved *proactively*. We can reduce the frequency and intensity of children's tantrums when we help them learn, in manageable increments, that disappointments are disappointments, not injustices, and there will be a next time.

In an important sense, all of the recommendations offered in this book—recommendations to strengthen positiveness in our relationships with our children; to repair moments of anger and misunderstanding; to help children bounce back, to think flexibly about solving problems, to compromise, and to take into account the needs of others—are solutions to the problem of a child's tantrums.

Many child therapists work on a daily basis with children who present severe problems of emotion regulation and behavioral control. These children often have biologically based qualities of temperament that increase both the intensity of their physical and emotional distress and the inflexibility of their behavioral reactions. They are often diagnosed with attention-deficit/hyperactivity disorder (ADHD), autistic spectrum disorders, mood disorders, or problems of sensory integration. These therapists have developed principles and techniques for reducing children's tantrums that are helpful for all children. I will describe many of these techniques, in addition to my own recommendations, throughout this chapter.

How Not to Have a Tantrum Back

Many years ago, the pediatrician T. Berry Brazelton, in a television interview, was asked how parents should respond to their children's tantrums. Brazelton offered this recommendation: "Don't have a tantrum back." Although this is often easier said than done, once a tantrum has begun, Brazelton's reply is still the essential advice.

Psychologists Ross Greene and J. Stuart Ablon have presented an excellent approach to the treatment of "explosive" children called "Collaborative Problem Solving," or CPS. In the CPS model, children's tantrums are understood to be the result of a delay in the development of important cognitive-emotional skills, especially the skills of frustration tolerance, flexibility, and problem solving.

To help children develop these skills, Greene and Ablon advise that parents first identify the "triggers" for a child's tantrums. In doing this, parents learn that tantrums are not random (as it often seems) but, rather, highly predictable. A child's explosiveness is then seen in a different light. It is no longer a behavior to be punished but, instead, "a problem to be solved."[1]

The problem-solving process includes several elements from the five essential steps I discussed in Chapter 8. Parents express empathy for their child's point of view and state, in a nonjudgmental way, their own concerns. Children are then engaged in problem solving. Recurring problematic situations are identified, alternative behaviors are discussed, and consequences are established.

The delineation of reasonable consequences for a child's misbehavior—brief punishments that are easily enforced—may be as important for us, as parents, as for our children. When you have a plan, when you know in advance the situations that are likely to trigger your child's tantrum and how you will respond, and when the consequences for your child's violations of rules have been clearly spelled out, you will more often be able to respond calmly (but still firmly), with less anger and retaliation, in these difficult moments. You should not try to think up consequences on the spot, or when you are angry, or at your wit's end.

Do not try to think up consequences on the spot, or when you are angry, or at your wit's end.

A Proactive Plan for Tantrums and Meltdowns

Set aside time, every day, for enthusiastic play and sharing of interests.

Every moment of interactive play is an experiential lesson in managing frustration and disappointment. Recall, for example, that preschool and kindergarten children in Tools of the Mind classrooms (Chapter 6) were not only more engaged in learning, they were also well behaved.

Inevitably, when we play with our children, there will be frustrations in the course of the play. The blocks will fall, or your child will not have exactly what he needs. And, at some time, before he would like, the play must end. These are teachable moments. We offer children both our empathy (we let them know that we understand their frustration and disappointment) and our problem-solving skills. We help them learn that, with our combined ingenuity and imagination, disappointments and frustrations can be overcome, and there will be a next time.

For children with severe difficulties in self-regulation and social engagement, Stanley Greenspan recommends that parents engage with their children in three to four 20-minute sessions of interactive play per day. For most parents of school-age children, this ideal is impractical. Other experts, however, have found that as little as 5 minutes a day is helpful.[2]

Set aside time, every day, for the repair of angry and critical interactions.

Use this time to talk about the frustrations and disappointments of the day. In these moments, make some effort to appreciate your child's point of view and to acknowledge his feelings and concerns, especially what he believes is unfair. If you are able to separate your child's *feelings* from his bad *behavior*, this is not as hard to do as it sometimes seems.

You can say, for example, "I know you were angry and upset today when I wouldn't let you buy a new toy." Or "I understand that you were disappointed when . . ." Or that "you felt left out when . . ." Or that "it wasn't fair when . . ."

Any plan to reduce children's tantrums will be more successful when a child feels that he has been heard. At least, he now knows that you know how he feels. He may still complain that "It's not fair," and we may still disagree. Often, however, you will find some truth in his complaint. And he may find some truth in yours.

When a child feels heard, we have reduced the urgency of his need—and set the stage for problem solving. In these moments, we begin to teach children a vocabulary for understanding and coping with urgent emotions. We also help prevent the buildup of anger and resentment, feelings that make the next meltdown more likely.

Lectures and long explanations will not be helpful. A simple acknowledgment of your child's feelings—and then some proactive problem solving—will be.

Reasoning with children about their tantrums—trying to convince them that hitting, demanding, or refusing to do what we ask are not effective strategies for getting what they want—may sometimes be necessary. But reason, by itself, will not be very helpful. Children already know this—because we have told them before. Pointing out to a child who refuses to do his homework that this is not a good thing for him in the long run will rarely help.

These discussions have their place, but much of our good advice goes out the window the next day, when he is, again, caught up in the emotion of the moment.

Anticipate.

This is a critical step in resolving children's tantrums. Although your child's meltdowns may sometimes seem unpredictable (parents often say, in their frustration, "We never know what is going to set him off"), this is only partly true. Most children have predictable triggers for meltdowns. At the very least, their tantrums are likely to occur at regular times of the day—when getting ready in the morning, when asked to turn off the television, when asked to wait, or when they lose at games. When you help your child anticipate these situations, times when he is likely to become frustrated or upset, you have begun the process of proactive problem solving.

Engage your child in proactive problem solving.

Solving tantrums—or any recurring behavior problem—begins the night before.

Most experts agree: Meltdowns cannot be solved "in the moment." The solution to the problem of tantrums and meltdowns is to develop a proactive plan that strengthens your child's planning, problem-solving, and emotion-regulation skills.

> **Solving tantrums—or any recurring behavior problem—begins the night before.**

Place the problem before your child and ask for her ideas. Brainstorm with her. Think of strategies—things that she can do when she has to wait, or when she is angry or upset. Ask your child what works for her. Tell her what works for you, when you are angry and upset.

These strategies may be simple skills, like taking deep breaths or taking a break from work; or they may be deeper, more lasting inner resources and calming strategies—learning to recall, for example, that painful feelings can be healed and that we all make mistakes.

Many young children find it helpful to go to a particular place in their room, an angry spot,[3] or play quietly with their dolls, action figures, and toys; their cards or iPod; or draw, or watch TV.

If your child's meltdowns involve waiting, plan activities he can do to make the waiting easier, activities he can do by himself—play with cards or draw, even Game Boy—until you are available.

If the problem is a feeling of disappointment, plan something he can look forward to, a "next time."

If the tantrum is a demand for things, establish a system of earning. Set aside a time for buying. Even when he has earned a new Lego set, he cannot have this when he wants it, but only on the day that has been set aside for buying.

If his tantrum involves aggressive behavior, teach him a different way to express anger and frustration. Practice and reward this new behavior. Behavioral research has demonstrated that oppositional and defiant children do not learn good behavior from lectures or from punishment. Instead, they learn from practice.[4]

Sometimes children will follow through on these specific suggestions, sometimes not. But your proactive planning has already been helpful. In these discussions, you have reduced the urgency and intensity of your child's needs and strengthened her problem-solving and emotion-regulation skills. She is likely, the next time, to make more effort at cooperation and self-control.

Do not demand more of your child than is reasonable.

Do not expect them to be able to wait, or to focus their attention, to follow through, to tolerate frustration, or to restrain their impulses, more than is reasonable. And what is reasonable for one child may not be reasonable for another. Children differ in their temperament and their capacity for self-control. Deciding what is reasonable to expect of a child requires knowing our children. As the child psychiatrist Stanley Turecki reminds us, expert parenting means being a different parent to different children.[5]

Reward good behavior.

Establish a system of earning. Children develop improved ability to accept delay when we reward—with praise or more tangible rewards—small improvements in their ability to wait without interrupting, making demands, or behaving aggressively. Praise for small increments in a child's effort is now recognized as an essential component of successful behavior change.

Tell your child, "When you are able to wait . . ." or "to stay calm . . ." or "When we have a good morning . . ." or "When you go to bed when I ask, then tomorrow, we will be able to have an extra game." These rewards, like everything else, are planned in advance. Do not offer rewards to your child once a tantrum has started. Instead, offer to listen—but only when he speaks to you calmly.

Rewards can be an opportunity to buy toys and games, but they can also be privileges, for example, a chance to stay up late or a day off from responsibilities.[6]

I may be among a minority of therapists in making the following recommendation: If a child calms down from a tantrum and speaks reasonably (not abusively) and if he is able to present some legitimate sense of urgency, parents should, on some occasions, give in to their child's request. I make this recommendation for two reasons: *(1)* because he has now made a *request* not a *demand* and *(2)* because allowing your child to feel heard in this way may support his subsequent engagement with you in finding proactive solutions, and this benefit outweighs the possible risk of reinforcing coercive tactics.

Waiting is especially hard for children with ADHD (and other children who are impulsive and strong willed). These children therefore need (and deserve) more frequent praise for waiting, even when they are only able to wait for short periods of time (for example, when you are on the phone). They deserve this praise because they have, in fact, worked hard.

Ask your child to make a small change.

Start with small changes.

Ask your child to make a small change. Acknowledge and reward his effort. If siblings are fighting, ask for a 24-hour moratorium on fighting and teasing. Most children can do this, if not the first day, then the second. Then work to extend the moratorium—first into a longer cease fire, then into a permanent peace agreement.

Speak to them calmly. Insist that they speak to you calmly.

This is another established principle of successful behavior change, recognized by all child therapists. Children are far more likely to respond to your limits and your requests when you are able to stay calm. When we yell, children may (sometimes) become afraid of our anger; more often, however, they do not. Anger, however justified, only makes children more defiant.

Give them a warning and give them time.

Do not expect immediate compliance. When you ask them to turn off the television, or to stop playing a video game, give them a 5-minute warning (and a short grace period after that).

Establish rules and consequences.

Almost universally, parents ask, "What punishment or consequence should I impose when my child throws the remote control, or screams and speaks abusively when I say, 'No?'"

In these situations, when a child's behavior goes over the line, consequences are necessary. It is important to remember, however, that consequences are a small part of the solution to children's tantrums. Self-regulation, especially in childhood, is not learned well from consequences. It is better learned through practice and praise.

In considering consequences, think baseball. As I mentioned in an earlier chapter, if a player curses at an umpire (parent), he is out of the game. If a player touches an umpire, he is suspended for three games. More egregious infractions, in both baseball and life (for example, inappropriate Internet behavior) may require longer suspensions (for example, the child loses all computer privileges and must earn them back).

Punishments are sometimes necessary. But serious behavior problems are never solved by punishments.

Consequences should usually be brief and easily enforced, for example, a brief time-out or the loss of an evening of screen time. If your child has been destructive, I suggest the following simple rule: If he has been destructive to objects (for example, if he has broken a toy) or to others (if he has said hurtful things), he must make restitution (for example, apologize) in some form.

Then, Reset.[7]

If a first punishment or consequence does not help change your child's behavior, more punishments, or more severe punishments, are even less likely to help. Don't "pile on" punishments.[8]

Don't punish your child first for hitting, then again for swearing as he walks away, then again for slamming the door to his room.

Although punishments are sometimes necessary, serious behavior problems are *never* solved by punishments.

More often than not, we punish our children because we don't know what else to do—and we feel that we have to do something. We don't want them to feel that they can act with impunity. And, in this, of course, we are right.

But, as many experts have pointed out, the threat of punishment is a small part of learning discipline and self-control. Frequent punishments have serious side effects, and these side effects often far outweigh whatever momentary compliance we might achieve.

As I have discussed previously, recent advances in behavior management programs increasingly emphasize praise for good behavior, with minimal use of punishment, in any form.

What children learn from punishment, at best, is to avoid punishment. And only this punishment, this time. At times, a child may learn to avoid punishment in a good way, for example, by studying or by not hitting. But frequent punishment also makes children angry and resentful. They will try to avoid the punishment, but they will not really change.

In the Moment

Calming children in the midst of a tantrum is often very difficult. We can sometimes de-escalate a tantrum with distraction or humor—but not always. We can sometimes calm a child with our recognition and acknowledgment of his frustration and disappointment—but not always. We can let him know that we know how he feels—that he *really* wants something, or *really* doesn't want something, that he *really* hates homework, and that he feels that our rules are unfair—but even these empathic statements will not always help. At times, there is only patience, calmness, and a firm insistence on behavior that is not destructive or hurtful to others. You should always be willing to listen to your child's complaint, but only "when you speak to me calmly."

When you are at your wit's end, you may even have to count to three.

Inevitably, they will sometimes win, and we will give in. But it is far from the worst parental sin if your child wins an argument and you decide to buy a toy or a souvenir he has been demanding, or let him watch an extra television program, or avoid a chore. In the real world, we cannot plan for every eventuality and we cannot be consistent all the time. Consistency, although perhaps an ideal to strive for, is overrated. If you give in once, you can always stay firm, with greater resolve, the next time.

A Review and Some Helpful Hints

- Anticipate: For most children, tantrums occur in response to predictable frustrations or at predictable times of the day.
- Do not demand more of your child than is reasonable. What is reasonable for one child may not be reasonable for another.
- Give your child a 5-minute warning.
- Proact. Before you go to the store, set the stage for her. Tell her what you are willing—and not willing—to buy or to do.
- Engage your child in problem solving: Ask for her ideas.
- Help your child make a small change in his behavior. Recognize and reward small improvements.

- Allow your child some expression of anger and defiance, as long as his behavior does not go over the line. Even then, give him a second chance. But not a third chance.
- Give him a signal that he is coming close to going over the line. The signal should be short and simple, for example, "John, remember."
- Think baseball. (You are the umpire.)
- If the tantrum is triggered by a frustration, give him something to look forward to, a "next time."
- If the tantrum is triggered by a demand for things, institute a system of earning.
- If the tantrum is triggered by a refusal to cooperate (for example, if she refuses to put away towels or clothes, or, in my office, to put away toys), do not move on to the next activity until the task is done.
- When saying, "No," or making a request, be physically close to your child. Children comply far less often when we shout our requests from the other side of the room.
- When you need to say, "No," don't just say, "No." Let your child know how and when he might be able to earn what he wants, and when you will be available to help him.
- At the end of every day, check in with your child and repair moments of anger and misunderstanding.

If these simple strategies for resolving a child's tantrums are not effective, ask why. You may need to look for deeper sources of frustration, discouragement, and resentment, and to your own behavior. An evaluation for a biologically based attention, mood, or learning disorder may be necessary.

Chapter 14

Winning and Losing

To help engage our child patients, child therapists have traditionally offered children an opportunity to play structured games—card games and board games, checkers or chess. Many children readily accept this offer. If the child is a boy, he is likely to eagerly anticipate these contests—and he will arrange to win, at least most of the time.

"Mommy, I Cheated, I Won"

Matthew was an enthusiastic but "impossible" 4-year-old boy—hyperactive and "noncompliant." Often during the course of the day, and especially when it was time to go to bed, Matthew simply would not listen. In exasperation, his parents, against their better judgment, had threatened to take away all his toys or send him to live with relatives.

In our first meeting, I asked Matthew whether he wanted to play a game, and he chose Candyland. Like so many children with whom I have played this first game of childhood, Matthew picked the cards he wanted from the deck, discarded those he didn't, and quickly landed on the winning square. He then ran excitedly into the waiting room to brag about his success: "Mommy, I cheated, I won."

Statements like this from a 4-year-old are charming, and most parents can tell similar tales of their young child's blithe indifference to rules. (And of the resentment and envy evoked in older siblings who have entered a new stage of development—the age of reality. When the parent of a 3-year-old expresses effusive praise for her child's early attempts at drawing, a 6-year-old sibling is likely to respond, "That's not beautiful, that's a scribble.")

But when magical play continues into the school years, we need to be concerned, because this problem in a child's social development is likely to have serious consequences—for his peer relationships and for his future emotional health. Getting along with others depends on learning to play by the rules.

How It Feels to Win and to Lose

Everyone who plays games with children quickly learns a first lesson: how important it is for them to win. For most children (and, to be honest, for many adults) these games *matter*. He does not *want* to win; he *needs* to win. Winning, by whatever means, evokes in young children a feeling of pride; losing evokes a feeling of failure and shame. These feelings are of critical importance in the lives of our children, especially young boys.

Losing, to all children, feels painful. To some children, losing feels catastrophic. Often it does not seem to matter whether the game is a game of skill or a game of chance. When he loses, he may throw game pieces, insist on a "do over," or refuse to play.

Many children who play in this way (like young Matthew), both boys and girls, are temperamentally impulsive and strong willed. It has therefore been more difficult for them to learn to control their expressions of frustration and disappointment, and they often respond to other disappointments (for example, losing a cap or being denied a treat or a souvenir) with the same catastrophic feeling as losing a game. Some younger children have not yet emerged from the age of illusion, the age when children are not yet expected to fully understand the idea of rules.

But, to be fair, we all get caught up in the game.

Losing and Demoralization

From a behavioral point of view, it may be said that children who cheat and brag have not learned mature social behavior, and this description is, of course, true. More fundamentally, however, these children feel, in some way, defeated. Winning and boasting offer them temporary relief from feelings of failure and envy.

Tom, an anxious 10-year-old boy, in one of our first sessions, asked to play chess. Tom won our first game. But, in the second game, I won. Tom became tearful. Despite my best efforts to offer support and understanding—about his good play and my many years of experience—Tom remained, for a long time, inconsolable. Later, I spoke with Tom's father about this experience. Mr. L told me that he had often observed the same reaction, especially when he played tennis with his son. Tom, he explained, was not yet good enough to beat him. When he loses, Tom often cries or becomes sullen, and he leaves the court, and Mr. L is highly critical of Tom for his immature behavior.

Tom's father, of course, is right; his son is not yet good enough to beat him (and Tom knows this) and Tom's behavior *is* immature. Still, I was taken aback at the unmitigated toughness of Mr. L's attitude. Tom felt defeated and demoralized. (In school, Tom was also demoralized because of learning problems.) Mr. L seemed not to have recognized this, and, as a result, Tom had become increasingly dismissive and defiant in his behavior toward his father.

I would object less, or perhaps not at all, if Mr. L had tempered the reality of his superiority with some effort to soften Tom's defeat, and if he had offered sincere appreciation of every advance that Tom made in his tennis (and academic) skills. Tom might then anticipate the day when he would win fairly, as did a somewhat older child, who told his father, with warmth and admiration, "I can't wait until I can beat you at tennis."

In the end, this may be what is most important: our encouragement and recognition of every increment of both effort and skill, when we play games with our children.

What Can We Do?

When you play games with your children, you need to appreciate the importance of a child's feeling of winning. (With very young children, you also need to remind yourself that, often, your child is not yet playing a game; his play lies somewhere in between fantasy play and a true game.) With this understanding as a guide, you will then be able to develop a good-natured, incremental approach to promoting your child's social development—his acceptance of rules and the rights of others.

In the course of playing a game, there will always be moments of excitement, anxiety, frustration, and disappointment. When you play with your children, if you play with enough enthusiasm and express some of your own excitement and disappointment, your child will also, in some way, acknowledge these feelings. These brief moments present an opportunity: You will observe how your child attempts to cope with frustration, and you can talk with him about it.

We help children with the problem of cheating, with winning and losing, when we help them cope with the anxiety, frustration, and disappointment that are part of every game—and everything we do.

Most children seem to benefit from talking about the disappointments and frustrations endured by their heroes, baseball players, for example, who sometimes strike out. (In baseball, as many writers have pointed out, even the best hitters fail twice as often as they succeed.) The goal of these discussions is to help children learn, in small increments, to tolerate disappointment—to help him learn that his disappointment is a disappointment, not a catastrophe, and that he will not *always* win or *always* lose.

If your child is involved in organized sports, I highly recommend, again, that you join Jim Thompson's Positive Coaching Alliance. Thompson's recommendations for coaches and parents offer wise alternatives to the frequent criticism and yelling that are so common in youth sports, and so destructive to children's enjoyment, motivation, and learning.

Our goal is to help children learn that a disappointment is a disappointment, not a catastrophe.

"A Little Fit, Not a Big Fit"

Michael was an enthusiastic and talented, but also perfectionistic, 9-year-old boy. Despite his many talents, Michael was easily upset. He would often cry in school, for example, if he made even a small mistake in his work. His parents (and I) had tried many ways to help Michael with this problem. We had talked with him about disappointments and frustrations, and tried to teach him that we all make mistakes. These sympathetic discussions had been helpful to Michael—but not helpful enough.

(It is always important to keep in mind the role of temperament in children's emotional and behavioral difficulties. Michael had an anxious temperament. His parents were neither too strict nor too permissive. They were caring and sympathetic but also capable of saying, "No.")

Recently, Mr. and Mrs. R had become increasingly frustrated and angry with Michael, when he began playing baseball. Michael explained, "When I strike out, I cry and have a big fit. Then my parents get really mad. They told me, if I don't stop, they won't let me play baseball. But I can't help it. I don't know what to do."

I said, "I know, a lot of times, kids get really upset when they strike out. Sometimes, grownups do to." But Michael had heard all this before. As I spoke, kindly and with empathy, he looked distracted. I asked Michael what he was thinking. He answered, sheepishly, but with refreshing honesty, "Actually, I was thinking, 'Blah, blah, blah.'"

I smiled and changed my tack. "OK, I have an idea. How about, if instead of having a big fit, you have a *little* fit. Walk to the side, away from your teammates, be upset for a minute, then come back." Michael looked surprised. This idea had not occurred to him. He told me, "No, that won't work. My parents will still be mad. They don't want me to have a fit at all." I said, "I know, but I think this will work. It takes time to learn how not to have a fit at all." Michael's parents agreed with this plan and Michael learned, gradually, to control his expressions of frustration and disappointment.

Should We Let Them Win?

I am often asked, by both parents and students, an unavoidable question: "Should I let him win?" The real question, of course, is not whether to let a child win, but when. With young children, knowing the pleasure this gives them, we let them win—we allow them to catch us when they chase us through the park, and to find us when we play hide and seek.

But at what age do we begin to insist on a real contest, to help children make the transition from illusion to reality. At what age do we play "our hardest"?

Over time, I have arrived at a simple, although controversial, answer: I let young children win, but not every time. (In therapy, and for parents as well, this decision often depends on an intuitive judgment—how fragile is this particular child, how easily discouraged, how gradual will his transition to real competition need to be?) Letting a child win does not teach a lack of respect for authority or encourage a denial of reality. It is an empathic recognition that kids are kids—and, being kids, they learn to accept disappointment, and the limitations of their own skills, gradually, through practice.

Let young children win, but not every time.

There are many ways to help children make this transition gradually. When playing games of skill, where we have superior knowledge and experience, we do not have to play our hardest. We can play with a handicap, or not play competitively at all, or point out to a child that he has made a bad move and let him take it back and try again. It is a sign of increasing maturity when a child tells us, "play your hardest," evidence of his acceptance of reality and his desire to "really" win (although, in the heat of the battle, he may still regress and, again, resort to cheating).

I recommend, above all, that parents play frequently and enthusiastically with their children. Then, allow your child to play "his way"—sometimes, but not every time. In these playful, competitive interactions, in innumerable small experiences of victory, followed by defeat, followed by victory, losing becomes tolerable.

What is even more important, I believe, is this: If you play often enough and with enough enthusiasm, with at least some attention to your child's pleasure in winning and some effort to soften his disappointment when he loses, the question of whether to let him win becomes less urgent. With each advance in his ability to tolerate disappointment, as his self-esteem is no longer shattered by losing, he becomes more open to our socializing influence, less insistent on playing *his* way, and eventually able to accept defeat gracefully.[1]

The Cheating Syndrome

When playing games, many young children take great pleasure in their victory—and in our defeat. To insure their victory, they make up their own rules, changing them for their purposes and to their advantage during the course of the game. Often they are not content with winning. They also engage in some expression of gleeful triumph—boasting, bragging, and taunting.[2]

Why do young children (especially young boys) so often need to play with us in this way? Why do they insist, not only on winning, but on gleeful triumph? Perhaps the answer to this question is simply that this is what young boys are like: Their jubilant behavior is an instinctive display of pride, an undisguised expression of a basic competitive need of human beings (both men and women)—to be better, in some way, than someone else. For young boys, the feeling of *winning*, the need to feel a sense of physical or intellectual dominance, to display their strength and skill, to feel strong in relation to other boys and men, seems essential to their self-esteem. Young children need to believe that they can, and will, do great things.

Developmental psychologist Susan Harter, based on her interviews with preschool children, reports this amusing, but important, finding:

> In the very young child, one typically encounters a fantasied self possessing a staggering array of abilities, virtues, and talents. Our preschool subjects, for example, gave fantastic accounts of their running and climbing capabilities, their knowledge of words and numbers, as well as their virtuosity in winning friends

and influencing others . . . fully 50% of them describe themselves as the fastest runner in their peer group.[3]

If we are honest, we will have to admit that a child's need for competitive triumph is never completely outgrown. As adults, our expressions of triumph and superiority (because of our fear of public disapproval) become more muted or disguised. But we are still allowed, and still need, to celebrate our victories.

The ability to accept defeat gracefully is not learned from instruction— it is learned through practice and the emulation of admired adults.

The problem of cheating (and gloating) is for us, as parents, a moral or behavioral problem. But for a child, it is more fundamentally an emotional problem. Your child cheats because, in that moment, he cannot bear the feeling of losing; he urgently needs to win, and you can help him most effectively if you understand the urgency of his feeling.

Many well-intentioned parents believe that this essential aspect of emotional maturity can be instilled through lectures and strict enforcement. My experience teaches a different lesson. The ability to accept defeat gracefully is not learned from instruction—it is learned through practice and the emulation of admired adults.

From the point of view of child development, especially the emotional health of a child, the philosophy of Vince Lombardi ("Winning isn't everything, it's the only thing") is profoundly wrong and teaches exactly the wrong lesson. Coach Carter offers a far more constructive philosophy than Coach Lombardi.

Yet this idea—that there is only winning and losing, and nothing else matters, highly questionable even in the realm of professional sports—seems to be making a resurgence among some social critics and parent advisors. These advisors believe that our children have become too soft, that they are in danger of losing their competitive drive, even that rewarding children for their participation—not for winning—somehow encourages the development of narcissism.

These ideas are silly. Children want to win. It is part of their instinctive endowment. When we offer prizes to all children, for their participation and their effort, we encourage participation and effort. I have never met a child who wanted to win any less, or tried any less hard, because he knew that everyone would be getting a prize. Children don't say, "I don't have to try hard, I'm going to get a trophy anyway." They want to win.

There is much more than winning that makes competition an important socializing experience: Children should learn from competition the importance of teamwork and cooperation, of commitment to others and respect for our opponents, and, especially, learning to play by the rules. Children need to learn that rules, whether in games or in families, in schools, and in other institutions, are not essentially arbitrary or capricious. Although they may sometimes seem arbitrary to children, rules are there for a reason. We need to demonstrate these reasons to our children.

If winning is everything, children will cheat.[4]

Chapter 15

Sleep, Television, and Electronic Games

Many children have difficulty going to sleep at night. A child may want her parents (or a sibling) to stay with her until she falls asleep. If we leave, she finds reasons to repeatedly call for us or come out of her room. She may (or may not) tell us about specific anxieties, for example, a fear of monsters or intruders; sometimes she "just feels scared." Over time, we are exhausted.

There are many causes for a child's difficulty falling asleep. Some children are anxious about going to school the next day. These children often present a Sunday night syndrome (not unlike some adults who are unable to fall asleep in anticipation of job-related stress) and they may go to sleep easily on weekend nights. Other children have become angry; their difficulty falling asleep reflects a (sometimes unconscious) preoccupation with angry thoughts. Or a child's difficulty going to sleep may have begun during a period of separation from her parents.

For the majority of children with sleep difficulties, however, we will be unable to find a specific cause. Their difficulty falling asleep is most likely the result of a biologically based anxiety sensitivity, an increased fear of separation or fear of the dark that is instinctive in all children. Even when we feel that we know the reason, or have developed a plausible explanation for a child's fear, this understanding may not help us solve the problem.

A Bedtime Plan

In helping a child fall asleep, parents should begin with all the common elements of a comforting bedtime routine: a regular bedtime, treasured dolls or stuffed animals, reading or telling a story, and time for your child to talk about any of her concerns—problems of the day or, especially, worries about the following day. Many children derive comfort from being able to help their dolls or stuffed animals (who may also be scared) feel better.

Despite these solacing rituals, however, your child may remain afraid and ask you to stay with her until she falls asleep. Some parents attempt to solve this problem by offering their child rewards for remaining in her room or punishments for leaving the room. In my experience, these strategies are rarely successful.

I recommend to parents a plan that helps almost all children learn to overcome nighttime separation anxiety. After your regular, comforting bedtime rituals, explain to your child that you will leave the room while she is going to sleep, but that you will come back, to check in on her, at regular intervals. Depending on your child's age and the intensity of her fear, return every 5 or 10 minutes, then at increasing intervals, over the course of the next few weeks. In this way, your child learns, in manageable increments, to tolerate being alone, because she anticipates your return.

Although she is afraid, she also wants to overcome her fear.

Almost all children cooperate with this plan because, although she is afraid, she also wants to overcome her fear. Some parents object to the initial increase in time and effort involved in this approach; but returning to check on your child requires less time and effort than responding (with increasing irritation) to her repeated questions and requests.

Of course, you must return as promised, before your child calls out or leaves her room; if you wait until she calls, she will have learned the wrong lesson. And although reward systems alone are usually unsuccessful in helping children overcome nighttime fears, you can add rewards as an additional incentive.

The Middle of the Night

The problem of children who wake up in the middle of the night and call out for us, or want to come into our bed, is more difficult to solve—and takes more time. You can help your child overcome this fear in the same way that you help her fall asleep at bedtime. The same principles apply—being comforted by and comforting to her dolls and stuffed animals and gradually learning to feel safe when she is alone in the dark. The only difference is that we are exhausted and unable to return to check on her, as we did earlier in the evening.

A temporary solution is therefore sometimes necessary: You can put a sleeping bag at the end of your bed for your child to use if she wakes up in the middle of the night. Most children are happy with this plan.

Then, as the going-to-sleep problem is resolved, the middle-of-the-night problem gradually fades as well. You can also add—as a final boost to your child's motivation—a special reward for staying in her room throughout the night.

Lack of Sleep and Its Effects on Children

The world feels different to us when we are tired. When we are tired, we become more anxious, more irritable, and more impatient. Problems that are easy to solve when we are rested, feel stressful, even overwhelming, when we are tired. We are also less able to inhibit and control our emotional reactions.

We have difficulty, especially, with tasks that require initiation, planning, and creativity, and persistence toward long-term goals. These, of course, are precisely the kinds of tasks we want our children to learn to do well.

When we are tired, we may think that we are getting by and doing okay. But we are not doing okay. We may be able to do rote tasks or exciting tasks, but not tasks that require us to consider alternatives, to react quickly and flexibly to unexpected events, and to keep more than one thing in mind.[1]

Many of our children may be chronically tired.

Po Bronson and Ashley Merryman report that, nationally, in their first year of high school, 60% of students are getting 8 hours of sleep; by their second year, only 30% are. Getting less than 8 hours of sleep doubles a student's chances of being diagnosed with clinical depression.

Several school districts in different parts of the country now start the school day an hour later, to help high school students get more sleep. The results have been dramatic. Students' motivation (and SAT scores) have gone up; levels of depression (and car accidents) have gone down.[2]

I have observed all of these effects of loss of sleep in my child and adolescent patients. In light of this research, I now more often make sleep a focus of therapy, especially with high school students.

Television and Electronic Games

The fascination of children and adolescents with electronic games, especially games with violent content, is the bane of many contemporary parents—and of increasing concern to scientists. As a therapist, I am often told, "All he wants to do is play his Game Boy or video games." Many teenagers (players and former players) openly acknowledge the addictive quality of these games, and they will tell us, when we ask, which games are more or less addictive.

Most often (although perhaps not always) a child's "addiction" to electronics is a symptom of some other underlying problem—an attempt (although he is unlikely to admit this) to find some distraction, or escape, from bad feelings.

The underlying problem might be feelings of discouragement or social isolation, or a family atmosphere of frequent conflict. These problems are often made worse by ineffective discipline. Here is a common pattern: Parents establish rules and children ignore them. Parents then admonish their children and threaten punishments but do not follow through.

Excessive screen time is also a frequent problem in families where both parents work extended hours and children are supervised by caregivers who lack the authority to enforce rules.

Although it is always important to address underlying problems, in the short term, we need a plan.

Many families have found the following guidelines helpful:

- Substitute interactive play for electronic play. Most children, despite some perfunctory protest, still prefer interactive play with a parent to watching television or playing video games, with all the benefits for their social and emotional development discussed throughout this book.
- Set aside a specified time for playing video games—and a time during which all electronics, including television, are turned off.
- I have also, at times, made what seems like a more radical proposal: Parents should play electronic games with their child. Watch your child play and ask him to teach you the game. This recommendation is an extension of the basic principle that we should express enthusiastic interest in our children's interests. Almost all children want their parents to watch them play these games, so they can show off their skill. The results of this informal experiment have been encouraging. Parents usually report, as predicted, that

taking a more active interest in their child's electronic games, and playing with them, does not encourage children to play these games more often. Instead, children are more willing, at a later time, to engage with their parents in interactive, nonelectronic play.

- Extra screen time can be earned as a reward for compliance with basic responsibilities.

Are Our Children Being Harmed by Violent Video Games?

In addition to the problem of the amount of time children spend in front of screens, scientific studies have raised serious concern about our children's exposure to media violence. Extensive research has established that frequent watching of violence on television and, especially, playing violent video games, is a risk factor for aggressive behavior in children and adolescents.

Children who watch violent television and play violent video games behave more aggressively in both laboratory and real-life situations. Playing violent video games has been shown to increase children's physiological arousal and to increase their aggressive thoughts, aggressive feelings, and aggressive behaviors. Children who frequently play these games are also, over time, less likely to be supportive and helpful to other children.[3]

Children who frequently play violent video games are less likely to be supportive and helpful to other children.

Fantasy play is different. Children who engage in make-believe play with well-developed plots—even when this play involves repeated battles among opposing forces—do not show more aggressive behavior.[4]

Children seem to learn from exposure to media violence that aggression is an acceptable—and successful—way to deal with conflicts, frustrations, and insults. Psychologists Dorothy and Jerome Singer point out that violence is ubiquitous in children's television programming, and that these programs rarely show the real-life costs and tragic consequences of violence.[5] Psychologist Craig Anderson and his colleagues also note that the graphic quality of the violence portrayed in video games has increased dramatically in the past decade.[6]

This research has also been able to answer the question of cause versus correlation. Contrary to my expectations, there is no evidence to support the hypothesis that aggressive children are more drawn to violent television and violent games. There is also no evidence for the idea that these activities provide a socially acceptable outlet for children's aggressive feelings.[7]

Why is it, then, that many children can play these games and are not influenced to behave aggressively? The answer is that media violence is one risk factor—among many risk and protective factors—in a child's life. Learning nonviolent methods of resolving conflicts is a protective factor. The risk and protective factor model (just like risk and protective factors for many physical diseases) helps explain why some children who play violent video games behave aggressively while others do not.

Based on this research, Craig Anderson and his colleagues offer some simple and reasonable recommendations with respect to media violence. We should limit our children's exposure to risk factors for aggressive behavior, including exposure to violent media, and promote protective factors. Especially, we should teach kids (by instruction and by example) constructive, non-aggressive ways of resolving conflicts. In addition, all of the recommendations presented in this book—recommendations to promote positive interactions, repair emotional injuries, and nurture children's social skills—can be thought of as efforts to strengthen protective factors in a child's emotional life.

PART III

Conclusion

Chapter 16

A Philosophy of Childhood and Final Take-Aways

In this final chapter, I would like to offer a brief review of lessons learned—lessons about childhood, about being a parent, about our relationships with our children, and about how we can foster our children's emotional health.

Parenthood begins with joy. Our joyfulness at the birth or adoption of a child, and at every succeeding milestone in our child's progress through life, is an instinctive expression of triumph—a triumph of hope over sadness and regret. In health, both parents and children are able to remain joyful and optimistic.

Childhood is, above all, a time of curiosity and wonder. Thomas Cole's simple but profound insight is for me the starting point for our understanding of children. Parents and parent advisors debate the nature of childhood and the needs of children. But despite our differences, there is much that we share: We all want our children to succeed in life—to do good things, to have good friends, to be good kids.

Children begin each day seeking enjoyment and feelings of pride, and wanting to share these feelings with others. They want to earn recognition and praise, especially from admired adults. They want to succeed, to win, to be the best. They want to have good feelings—not only about themselves but also about others. They want to feel secure in our love and to be accepted by their peers.

Children are not lazy or manipulative. If they have become manipulative or appear lazy, these are symptoms of deeper problems. Every child, no matter how angry or discouraged, no matter how defiant, secretive, or unmotivated he may seem to be, at the same time wants our approval and wants to do well.

Our children look up to us. Because they look up to us, they want to be, and to become, like us. They want to do what we are able to do, to know as much as we know, and to be looked up to by others. And because they look up to us, our pride in their character and their accomplishments remains important, throughout their lives.

Children are idealistic. They believe that anything is possible, and that we, their parents, know everything and can do anything. In health, some of this idealism should remain.

Of course, children are also mischievous, impulsive, and strong willed; jealous and egocentric; demanding and sometimes cruel. They protest—loudly and vehemently—when they do not get what they want, and when they believe that our restrictions on their freedom are unfair. Therefore, children need guidance and limits. Our children need to know that their feelings are important, but so are the needs and feelings of others.

It is not either/or. We should encourage their self-expression and *also* teach them self-restraint. Our love is unconditional. But their success in life, and the things that they want, are earned—through initiative, responsibility, and hard work.

Emotional Health

Psychological health, in childhood and throughout life, depends on our ability to hold onto positive emotions and positive *expectations*. Children with positive expectations for their futures will more often make good decisions in the present. They will also more readily accept our discipline, because they will understand the need for it.

Children thrive in an atmosphere of positiveness and encouragement. They seek—and need—our enthusiastic responsiveness to their expressions of interest and their prideful display of their emerging skills. Children need our appreciation—and, yes, our praise—for their efforts and for the good things that they do. Just as we all do.

Resilience

Like us, children face challenges—moments of discouragement and frustration, disappointment and sadness. In health, they are able to bounce back. In unhealthy development, children do not quickly bounce back. They remain, longer than they should, demoralized, angry, and alone.

In health, children learn that bad feelings do not last forever. They learn that they can make things better, that they will do better the next time, and there are other good things to look forward to.

These are critical moments in the emotional life of a child—when admired adults find a way to help a sad, anxious, or angry child realize that she will not always feel this way; when we are able to help a child who is disappointed or discouraged regain some measure of confidence in her future.

When we are able to help children bounce back, we set in motion a fulcrum shift in their emotional development—a shift that leads *away* from urgent and insistent demands and *toward* initiative, problem solving, and acceptance of personal responsibility. Children who are able to bounce back will engage in life with a sense of purpose, and they will want to learn what we have to teach.

We strengthen our children's emotional resilience with our empathy, encouragement, and support. When they are excited, we share their excitement. When they are anxious, frustrated, or disappointed, we offer solace and understanding. Then, we help them solve problems. We teach them that problems can be solved and that painful disappointments do not last forever.

We try to understand what is important to them—and then teach them what is important to us. And we let them know that we know how they feel, because we have also had these feelings. At the end of the day, there is no more important parenting skill than patient listening, and nothing that we do as parents that is more important to our children's success in life.

Empathy and understanding remain the essence of good parenting.

Character

But even our enthusiasm and our empathy are not enough.

We accept, as parents, a fundamental responsibility: to provide our children with a practical and a moral education. We need to prepare them for the challenges and responsibilities they will face as adults.

Children need to learn to control their aggression, to play by the rules, and to be able to make and keep friends. We want them to be responsible, to consider the needs of others, and to learn the importance of hard work.

Many parents believe that children learn to behave responsibly when they know what is expected of them and when they come to understand the consequences of their actions. There is, of course, some truth in this idea. But only some. Children who are angry and discouraged will not behave well, regardless of the consequences of their actions.

Social skills are best learned in the course of playful interactions. They are not learned in front of a screen, and they are not learned through lectures or admonishments.

When we play and work with our children, children come to understand and accept, deeply and for the right reasons, that rules are necessary—for safety and for living with others.

We foster our children's character development when we treat them—and each other—with respect, when we resolve our conflicts through reasoning and discussion, and when we let them know that we are proud of them, especially for the good things they do for others.

As parents, our moral influence with our children is ultimately based on respect.

Criticism

We are, unwittingly, too critical of our children. This judgment is based on my personal clinical experience and supported by scientific research.

We all know, from our own lives, how criticism feels. We may have experienced the demoralizing effects of frequent criticism in the workplace or in our love relationships. Why do we so often fail to consider this in relation to our children?

Much of our criticism is well intentioned. We criticize because we are anxious about our children's futures. We want them to improve, and eventually succeed in a competitive world. When we are critical, we believe that we are doing the right thing. We regard our child's defiance (or his unwillingness to communicate) as an unavoidable consequence of responsible parenting. It is not.

We need to understand how hurtful our words can be.

There is no better antidote to frequent criticism than patient listening. Listening, of course, does not mean agreement or giving in to unreasonable demands. When we listen, we make a genuine effort to understand our child's point of view, to appreciate his efforts at cooperation, and to acknowledge what is *right* about what he is saying before we point out what is *wrong*.

Expressions of appreciation are remarkably helpful in beginning to repair angry and hurtful interactions. In this effort, it is important for us, as parents, to take the lead. Isn't this what "be the parent" should really mean?

Motivation

Parents often ask, "Why isn't he more motivated?" "Why doesn't he seem to care?" The answer to these questions is almost always, "Because he is discouraged." It is easier for him to pretend that he doesn't care. Children say that they don't care—but they do care.

All constructive activity involves moments of anxiety, frustration, and discouragement. Our ability to sustain effort at any task requires some confidence in our eventual success and some feeling of accomplishment or progress along the way.

We strengthen our children's motivation when we respond with enthusiasm to their interests and projects, even when these are not the interests we would choose, and when we make note of every *improvement*, not every *mistake*.

Like inspiring teachers, we need to listen for the great sound or the creative idea. Recall William Damon's wise advice: "Listen closely for the spark, then fan the flames."

Communication

So often, our children seem reluctant to talk to us, even to report mundane events of the day. Why is this so?

A child's silence is an instinctive self-protective behavior, evoked by the anticipation of painful feelings. Children do not want to talk to us when they feel ashamed; or when they are afraid that we will be critical; or when they believe that talking will just make them feel bad all over again, or feel worse.

When we ask a child a question, often he has come to hear more than our question. He knows that many of our neutral questions are not really neutral. He may wonder, why are you asking me about *this*?

There are answers to these problems, but there is no magic.

Communication begins, again, with interest. Then, listen to her grievances. Find out what she feels is unfair in her life.

Give her time. Hang out with her. Be personal. Repair moments of anger and criticism.

If we are willing to acknowledge *our* mistakes, our children will be more likely to own up to theirs.

Behavior

"Why does he keep acting this way?" "Why does he tease and hit his sister?" "Why does he continue to lie when we know that he is lying?" "Why, when I've told him so many times, does he still refuse to listen?" "Is he just trying to get attention?"

The answer is, "He acts this way because he is caught up in the emotion of the moment." As we all are, at times.

Children do not misbehave because they are trying to make us angry or push our buttons. Children misbehave because, in the first place, they are being kids.

It seems almost instinctive for many parents to respond to their child's bad behavior by imposing (or threatening) a punishment or consequence. Persistent behavior problems, however, are not solved by punishments (or by lectures). Occasional punishments have their place, but they are not the best way to promote good behavior in children.

If we want our children to be well behaved, we should play (and work) with them often. This is the best way to teach them cooperation and self-restraint. The best way to help children learn to cooperate, when there is work that needs to be done, is to work with them.

When we talk with our children, we should speak to them calmly, and we should speak respectfully to each other. If we are frequently angry and critical, our children will not be well behaved, no matter how much discipline we provide.

Then, we can let them know when their behavior is over the line—and we can take a time-out. But it is really a time-out, with an opportunity to start over, to try again, to do better the next time.

Children who are impulsive and strong willed will require more patience *and* more firmness, more opportunities to practice self-restraint, more frequent praise for every increment of effort and helpfulness, and more moments of repair.

Solving Problems

Children want to solve problems. Like us, however, they may become frustrated and stubborn, defensive and blaming of others. And, like us, they may just not know what to do.

The first step in solving any family problem is to take a step back. Problems of family life are best solved proactively. Look for causes, not just symptoms. Listen to your child's point of view. Engage him in the search for solutions. Then develop a plan.

When we engage children in the solution of a problem, they become less absorbed in angry and defiant thoughts, less stuck in making demands or continuing the argument. They begin to think, even if just for that moment, less about how to get their way and, instead, about how to solve a problem.

What Matters Most

Over time, I have come to a personal philosophy and some simple conclusions about being a parent. I believe that what matters most in our children's emotional development—and to their success in life—is not how strict or how permissive we are, but our children's inner certainty of our interest, encouragement, and support.

Our constant presence in the lives of our children as a source of emotional support is, I believe, our most essential task as parents, and continues throughout their lives.

We support our children's emotional health when we share their joys and offer solace for their sadness and disappointments, and when we are willing to repair the conflicts that occur, inevitably, in our relationships.

Our children's confident expectation of our recognition and approval—that we are proud of them and believe they are capable of doing good things—sustains them during inevitable moments of anxiety and self-doubt.

In these ways, we strengthen our children's inner resources and we become an inner presence—a voice of encouragement *and* moral guidance.

We will then observe this healthy development in all areas of our children's lives—in better peer relationships, in less urgent and inflexible demands, and in less frequent avoidance and withdrawal—overall, a more confident, more joyful, and more responsible engagement in life.

NOTES

Introduction

1. Stout, H. (2009). For Some Parents, Shouting Is the New Spanking. *New York Times*, October 21, 2009.

2. Senior, J. (2010). All Joy and No Fun: Why Parents Hate Parenting. *New York Magazine,* July 12, 2010. See also Warner, J. (2005). *Perfect Madness: Motherhood in the Age of Anxiety*. New York: Riverhead Books.

3. Blow, C. (2010) Friends, Neighbors and Facebook. *New York Times*, June 11, 2010. See also Glenn, H. S., and Nelson, J. (2000). *Raising Self-Reliant Children in a Self-Indulgent World*. New York: Three Rivers Press.

4. The anthropologist Sarah Hrdy has recently presented evidence to support the thesis that the help of others in raising children played a critical role in human evolution. Hrdy argues that communal involvement in the care of children fostered the growth of our unique capacities for communication and mutual understanding, and that these capacities—to care about what others think and feel—then made possible our subsequent achievements in culture and technology, and our survival as a species. Hrdy, S. (2009). *Mothers and Others*. Cambridge, MA: Harvard University Press.

5. When my children were young, Thomas Gordon's *Parent Effectiveness Training* was among the most popular guides for parents (see Gordon, T. 1970. *Parent Effectiveness Training*. New York: Three Rivers Press). I have (belatedly) read Dr. Gordon's book. Although Gordon's ideas have been the subject of recent criticism from advocates of more consistent

discipline and greater parental authority, some of his recommendations, especially on the importance of active listening and problem solving, have entered the common wisdom of parenting. (Gordon advises, for example, that we should avoid "You-messages," which are accusatory and evoke a child's defensiveness, and, instead, use "I-messages" that directly communicate our feelings and concerns.) As a young parent, however, it did not occur to me to read this book. I did not aspire to be an *effective* parent. I wanted to be a *good* parent—the kind of father who would earn my children's love and respect, as my parents had earned mine. And I could not imagine how these qualities of being a parent could be "trained."

6. Russert, T. (2006). *Wisdom of Our Fathers*. New York: Random House, pp. 22–23.

7. This simple anecdote also contains the essential answer to those who assert, based on research in behavior genetics, that parents have limited influence on the lives of their children (Harris, J. R. 1998. *The Nurture Assumption*. New York: Simon and Shuster). The love and support that Ms. Hackett feels from her father, poorly measured by social science, is the result of nurture, not nature, and of profound importance in its own right.

Chapter 1

1. Powell, E. A. (1990). *Thomas Cole*. New York: Harry N. Abrams, Inc.

2. For more detailed discussions of the emotion of interest, see Frijda, N. (2007). *The Laws of Emotion*. Mahwah, NJ: Lawrence Erlbaum Associates; Izard, C. (1991). *The Psychology of Emotions*. New York: Plenum Press; Izard, C. E., and Ackerman, B. P. (2000). Motivational, Organizational, and Regulatory Functions of Discrete Emotions. In M. Lewis and J. M. Haviland-Jones (Eds.), *Handbook of Emotions* (2nd ed.). New York: Guilford Press, pp. 253–264; and Panksepp, J. (1998). *Affective Neuroscience*. Oxford, UK: Oxford University Press.

3. Russell, B. (1930). *The Conquest of Happiness*. London: Routledge Classics, p. 110.

4. Schore, A. (1994). *Affect Regulation and the Origin of the Self*. Hillsdale, NJ: Lawrence Erlbaum Associates.

5. For a recent experimental study of the nature of interest, see Silvia, P. J. (2005). What Is Interesting? Exploring the Appraisal Structure of Interest. *Emotion*, 5(1), 89–102.

6. Buechler, S. (2008). *Making a Difference in Patients' Lives: Emotional Experience in the Therapeutic Setting*. New York: Routledge, p. 115.

7. This study is discussed in Seligman, M. (2002). *Authentic Happiness*. New York: Simon and Shuster.

8. Vaillant, G. (2002). *Aging Well.* New York: Little, Brown and Company

9. Schore, A. (1994).

10. See Fredrickson, B. (2001). The Role of Positive Emotions in Positive Psychology: The Broaden-and-Build Theory of Positive Emotions. *American Psychologist*, 56(3), 218–226.

11. And their importance in human relations generally. In benign or malignant forms, the emotions of pride and shame are critical determinants of human attitudes and behavior. An essential aspect of the appeal of many tyrants, for example, despite their ruthlessness, is their ability to undo feelings of humiliation and provide a renewed sense of national or ethnic pride.

Emotion theorists refer to pride and shame as "self-conscious" or "self-evaluative" emotions, because self-evaluation is intrinsic to our experience of pride and shame. In childhood, these self-evaluations—what children feel they are "good at" or "not good at"; whether they are liked or disliked, accepted or excluded—are continually present, very close to, if not synonymous with, what we loosely call self-esteem.

12. Students often ask about the difference between shame and guilt. Although there are several differences between these related emotions, the most essential difference is this: We feel guilt "about *things* done or not done in the world"; shame, in contrast, involves "the whole *self*. It is the vicarious experience of the other's scorn of the self." Lewis, H. B. (1989). Some Thoughts on the Moral Emotions of Shame and Guilt. In L. Cirillo, B. Kaplan, and S. Werner (Eds.), *Emotions in Ideal Human Development*. Hillsdale, NJ: Lawrence Erlbaum Associates, pp. 40–41.

13. In his studies of emotion, Darwin wrote that shame is most often evoked by "blame, criticism and derision." (Cited in Izard, C., 1991, p. 338.)

14. Gilbert, P. (2003). Evolution, Social Roles, and the Differences in Shame and Guilt. *Social Research*, 70(4), 1205–1230; Gilbert, P., and McGuire, M. T. (1998). Shame, Status, and Social Roles: Psychobiology and Evolution. In P. Gilbert and B. Andrews (Eds.), *Shame: Interpersonal*

Behavior, Psychopathology, and Culture. New York: Oxford University Press, pp. 99–125.

15. Holodynski, M. (2009). *From Social to Self-Evaluating Emotions: The Facilitating Role of Adults in the Emergence of Pride and Shame*. Paper presented at Society for Research in Child Development, Denver, Colorado, April 2009.

Children experience shame early in life. If we present puzzles to 3-year-old children that are too difficult for them to solve, they will look downward and away from us and their bodies will collapse, with their shoulders falling in. Empathic adults—and often other children, even empathic chimpanzees—recognize this emotional state and instinctively offer "consolations" to the child; we put our arm around her shoulder, to mitigate her feeling of shame (DeWaal, F., 2001. *The Ape and the Sushi Master*. New York: Basic Books).

A child's feeling of pride can also be observed early in childhood. As early as age 18 months, children smile after completing a task. Even earlier, infants show joy and delight "as the result of having some effect on the environment or . . . exercising some emerging skill." It is likely that these experiences of mastery or success, of "making things happen," represent an early form of pride. Unambiguous expressions of pride—for example, smiling *and* turning to look at an adult following the successful completion of a task—are reliably observed when children are between 2 and 3 years old. Stipek, D. (1995). The Development of Pride and Shame in Toddlers. In J. P. Tangney and K. W. Fischer (Eds.), *Self-Conscious Emotions: The Psychology of Shame, Guilt, Embarrassment, and Pride*. New York: The Guilford Press, pp. 237–252.

16. Weisfeld, G. E. (1997). Discrete Emotions Theory With Specific Reference to Pride and Shame. In N. L. Segal, G. Weisfeld, and C. C. Weisfeld (Eds.), *Uniting Psychology and Biology: Integrative Perspectives in Human Development*. Washington, DC: American Psychological Association, p. 426.

17. Tracy, J. L., and Robins, R. W. (2007). The Nature of Pride. In J. L. Tracy, R. W. Robins, and J. P. Tangney (Eds.), *The Self-Conscious Emotions: Theory and Research*. New York: The Guilford Press, p. 264.

18. Tracy, J. L., and Robins, R. W. (2007).

19. A recent book by psychologists Jean Twenge and W. Keith Campbell, for example, argues that overpraising our children has contributed to a "narcissism epidemic." Twenge, J. M., and Campbell, W. K. (2009).

The Narcissism Epidemic. New York: Simon and Shuster. See also Damon, W. (1995). *Greater Expectations*. New York: The Free Press; Seligman, M. (1995). *The Optimistic Child*. Boston: Houghton Mifflin; Kindlon, D. (2001). *Too Much of a Good Thing*. New York: Hyperion; and Young-Eisendrath, P. (2008). *The Self-Esteem Trap*. New York: Little, Brown and Company.

20. In a study that has special relevance for parents, Mueller and Dweck report that children who were praised for their *intelligence*, rather than for their *effort*, showed less persistence and less enjoyment when they were presented with challenging problems at a later time. Mueller, C. M., and Dweck, C. (1998). Intelligence Praise Can Undermine Motivation and Performance. *Journal of Personality and Social Psychology*, 75, 33–52.

21. Dweck, C., and Elliott-Moskwa, E. (2010). Self-Theories: The Roots of Defensiveness. In J. Maddux and J. P. Tangney, *Social Psychological Foundations of Clinical Psychology*. New York: The Guilford Press, pp. 136–153.

22. At stressful times, college students with a fixed mindset are more likely to become depressed, to be self-critical, and to ruminate about their problems. Students with a growth mindset more often take constructive action in response to the stresses they encounter. Dweck, C. (2006). *Mindset: The New Psychology of Success*. New York: Random House. See also Dweck, C. (2002). The Development of Ability Conceptions. In J. S. Eccles and A. Wigfield (Eds.), *Development of Achievement Motivation*. San Diego, CA: Academic Press, pp. 57–88.

23. Dweck, C. (2006), pp. 170–173.

24. Bronson, P., and Merryman, A. (2009). *Nurture Shock*. New York: Twelve, p. 24.

25. Kohn presents several reasons why the use of rewards, including praise, may be harmful to children. He believes that praise (and other rewards for good behavior) is a form of what he calls *conditional love*. In Kohn's view, when we praise our children (when we say to them, for example, "Good job!"), these statements often convey an implicit message that they are loved "conditionally," that is, only when they behave the way we want them to. (Kohn explains, "It's a way of saying to children: 'You have to jump through my hoops in order for me to express support and delight.'")

Kohn also objects to praise on philosophical grounds. He believes that, in most instances, praise, whether it is given by parents, by teachers, or in the work setting, is a method of control, used for the benefit of the person in power—the person who *gives* the rewards, not the one who *receives* them; in our case, for the benefit of adults, not children.

Kohn presents these ideas as an argument against a behaviorist approach to parenting, based on rewards and punishments. In my opinion, Kohn's anti-behaviorism goes too far. Approval and disapproval, praise and even occasional punishment, are unavoidable in raising children. These methods have their place in the behavioral development—and inner life—of every child.

We need to recognize a basic tension in our concerns as parents. Even if we reject a child-rearing philosophy based on excessive control, we cannot evade our socializing responsibility. All responsible parents want to promote prosocial values in their children. We feel proud of our children when we see them spontaneously offer comfort to a child who has been hurt or when they have worked hard on a difficult task, and we are appreciative when they help us (for example, by cleaning their room or going to bed on time) when they would rather have been doing something else. We want to promote these values as part of our children's character. When we tell them that we are proud of them or that we appreciate their help, this is perhaps a form of control, but it is a reasonable and inescapable one. It is not conditional love.

See Kohn, A. (1993). *Punished by Rewards: The Trouble With Gold Stars, Incentive Plans, A's and Other Bribes*. New York: Houghton Mifflin; and Kohn, A. (2005). *Unconditional Parenting*. New York: Simon and Shuster.

26. Reiss, S., Silverman, W., and Weems, C. (2001). Anxiety Sensitivity. In M. W. Vasey and M. R. Dadds (Eds.), *The Developmental Psychopathology of Anxiety*. New York: Oxford University Press, pp. 92–111. See also Biederman, J., Rosenbaum, J. F., Bolduc-Murphy, E. A., Faraone, S., Chaloff, J., Hirschfeld, D. R., and Kagan, J. (1993). Behavioral Inhibition as a Temperamental Risk Factor for Anxiety Disorders. *Child and Adolescent Psychiatric Clinics of North America*, 2, 667–684.

27. Izard, C. (1991).

28. Over the past two decades, effective cognitive-behavioral strategies have been developed to reduce children's anxiety. These techniques help children cope with anxiety in several ways. Children learn to reevaluate their anxious thoughts, and they are taught relaxation techniques to

reduce the physiological arousal associated with anxiety. They are encouraged to limit their worries to a particular time of the day (for example, to put aside a "worry time") and to practice assertive, problem-solving thoughts and behaviors. They are encouraged to plan something to look forward to and to gradually expand their comfort zones (for example, their ability to be alone or to try a new food), and they receive recognition and praise for every small step they are able to take toward these goals. See Kendall, P., and Suveg, C. (2006). Treating Anxiety Disorders in Youth. In P. C. Kendall (Ed.), *Child and Adolescent Therapy* (3rd ed.). New York: The Guilford Press, pp. 243–294. See also Chansky, T. (2004). *Freeing Your Child From Anxiety*. New York: Broadway Books.

29. Lemerise, E. A., and Dodge, K. A. (2000). The Development of Anger and Hostile Interactions. In M. Lewis and J. M. Haviland-Jones (Eds.), *Handbook of Emotions* (2nd ed.) New York: Guilford Press, pp. 594–606.

30. Expressions of anger can be reliably observed in infancy at 3 or 4 months of age. These early facial expressions of anger occur in response to arm restraint or inoculations (Lemerise, E. A., and Dodge, K. A., 2000). And it stays this way. Throughout life, pain and injury (especially when we believe that our pain or injury has been intentionally inflicted) and restraint on our freedom of movement, our ability to do what we want, what we feel we are entitled to do, remains a primary source of anger.

31. See, for example, Lochman, J. E., Powell, N. R., Whidby, J. M., and Fitzgerald, D. P. (2006). Aggressive Children: Cognitive-Behavioral Assessment and Treatment. In P. C. Kendall (Ed.), *Child and Adolescent Therapy* (3rd ed.). New York: The Guilford Press, pp. 33–81; and Greenberg, M. (2006). Promoting Resilience in Children and Youth: Preventive Interventions and Their Interface With Neuroscience. In M. Lester, A. Masten, and B. McEwan (Eds.), Resilience in Children. *Annals of the New York Academy of Sciences*, 1094, 139–150.

32. Panksepp, J. (1998).

33. Keller, H. (1984). *Geraldine's Blanket*. New York: Greenwillow Books.

34. Miller, M. (1987). *My Grandmother's Cookie Jar*. Los Angeles: Price, Stern, Sloan, Inc.

Chapter 2

1. On the importance of emotion regulation, see, especially, Gottman, J. M., Katz, L., and Hooven, C. (1997). *Meta-Emotion: How Families Communicate Emotionally*. Mahwah, NJ: Lawrence Erlbaum Associates; Graziano, P. A., Reavis, R. D., Keane, S. P., and Calkins, S. D. (2007). The Role of Emotion Regulation in Children's Early Academic Success. *Journal of School Psychology*, 45, 3–19; Blair, C. (2002). School Readiness: Integrating Cognition and Emotion in a Neurobiological Conceptualization of Children's Functioning at School Entry. *American Psychologist*, 57(2), 111–127; and Blair, C., and Diamond, A. (2008). Biological Processes in Prevention and Intervention: The Promotion of Self-Regulation as a Means of Preventing School Failure. *Development and Psychopathology*, 20, 899–911.

In contrast, emotion *dysregulation* is a core feature of, and a proven risk factor for, behavioral and emotional problems at all ages. See Keenan, K. (2000). Emotion Dysregulation as a Risk Factor for Child Psychopathology. *Clinical Psychology: Science and Practice*, 7(4), 418–434; and Bradley, S. (2000). *Affect Regulation and the Development of Psychopathology*. New York: Guilford Press.

2. Panksepp, J., and Burgdorf, J. (2003). "Laughing" Rats and the Evolutionary Antecedents of Human Joy? *Physiology and Behavior*, 79, 533–547; quote is from p. 533.

3. The philosopher Martha Nussbaum notes that our emotions are always about important things. She calls these our "projects"; the psychologist Nico Frijda calls them our "concerns." Nussbaum, M. (2001). *Upheavals of Thought: The Intelligence of Emotions*. New York: Cambridge University Press. See also Frijda, N. (2007). *The Laws of Emotion*. Mahwah, NJ: Lawrence Erlbaum Associates.

4. Mogel, W. (2001). *The Blessing of a Skinned Knee*. New York: Penguin Books, p. 36.

5. Damon, W. (1995), p. 102.

6. Many other social critics agree. Cultural critic Kay Hymowitz, for example, believes that contemporary parents, influenced by permissive parent advisors, have abdicated their responsibility to transmit culture and moral values. She describes our current child-rearing philosophy as "anticultural." Hymowitz argues that, unlike previous generations of parents, who regarded children as instinctively egoistic and therefore needing to learn discipline and restraint, we now imagine our children

to have an instinctive empathy and moral intelligence, and therefore needing minimal instruction and moral guidance. Our children, Hymowitz believes, are now "taught to seek meaning and value only from the inside . . . They are citizens not so much of a society as of their own undernourished imaginations." Hymowitz, K. (1999). *Ready or Not*. New York: The Free Press, p. 19.

7. Damon, W. (1995), p. xiii. See also Young-Eisendrath, P. (2008).

8. Belkin, L. (2009). A New Look at Overparenting. *New York Times*, November 19, 2009.

9. Dan Kindlon begins his thoughtful critique of parental indulgence with the case of highly successful parents who are less concerned about their adolescent son's plagiarism, substance abuse, defiant attitudes, and reckless driving than about the grades on his high school transcript. Getting into a "good college" is all that seemed to matter to these parents. In this case, Kay Hymowitz would certainly be right: These parents have sacrificed their son's citizenship to "the god of individual achievement."

Wendy Mogel cites the case of a public high school that, following the death of one of its students, provided grief counseling for other students but no organized effort to help the grieving family. This example is particularly instructive, because it is likely that the best form of grief counseling for these students would be, in fact, not only to express their own feelings but to offer help to the family of the student who had died.

10. In Damon's words, "the loss of all obligation to serve anyone beyond oneself" (Damon, W., 1995, p. 38).

11. These trends are documented and discussed in Twenge, J. (2006). *Generation Me*. New York: Free Press; and in Seligman, M. E. P. (1995).

12. Where I live and work, for example, when siblings continually argue about what television programs to watch (even in the era of easy recording), many affluent parents, instead of insisting that their children learn to compromise and take turns, prefer "the Westchester solution." Each child is given his own television, which he can watch in his own room. In his 2001 survey of parenting practices among affluent families, Dan Kindlon reports a similar observation: In over 50% of these families, each child had a television in his bedroom. This is indulgence. But it is not indulgence based on overconcern for a child's feelings; it is indulgence for our convenience.

To be frank, I have also met some irresponsible parents. Many of Damon's examples of poor parenting are not cases of parents who are indulgent or permissive, but rather, irresponsible and disengaged. The parents of Kindlon's adolescent patient who condone his plagiarism might be called "indulgent," but this young man's problems have deeper causes. Shouldn't we ask, why is he so reckless and dishonest in the first place?

13. Damon, for example, acknowledges the crucial importance of empathy in the successful socialization of children, a process he refers to, in a helpful formulation, as "bridge building." He expresses concern, however, that "our heightened concern with children's internal mental states" may encourage children's self-centeredness, undermine "objective moral referents," and convey an implicit message that the child's needs always come first, "putting the child at the center of all things" (Damon, W., 1995, p. 78).

14. These philosophies also correspond to the major dimensions of parental behavior identified by Diana Baumrind in her classic, and much debated, research on the optimal socialization of children. Baumrind found that parents could be distinguished on two basic dimensions of parenting behavior: parental *responsiveness* and parental *demandingness*. In these studies, parents of the most responsible and socially mature children were high in *both* responsiveness *and* demandingness. Baumrind referred to this style of parenting as *authoritative*, in contrast to *authoritarian* or *permissive*, parenting. Baumrind, D. (1989). Rearing Competent Children. In W. Damon (Ed.), *Child Development Today and Tomorrow*. San Francisco: Jossey-Bass, pp. 349–378.

15. Psychologist Theodore Dix has presented the most helpful framework I know of for understanding these dilemmas. Dix explains that, in any given instance, our decisions as parents are influenced by competing goals and concerns. When we are guided by *empathic* goals, we focus our attention on what children want—on helping them, at that moment, feel happy or feel better. To achieve empathic goals, parents need to understand their child's subjective state. We therefore monitor our child's facial, vocal, and postural cues; we make inferences about what she may be thinking and feeling, and about how we can console and comfort her.

When we are guided by what Dix calls *socialization* goals, we focus our attention on what we want *for* our children. We attempt to foster behaviors in our children that we believe will benefit them, now and in the future—behaviors that we believe are right but that children may not, at that moment, want. We insist, for example, on sharing and on going to bed on time.

At other times, we are motivated by what Dix calls *self* goals. Self goals are not necessarily selfish. Our needs to go to work and to get a good night's sleep, for example, are self goals, and these needs may compete with either our empathic or our socialization goals. Parents bring multiple goals to most situations involving their children. As our stress increases, however, the importance of self goals also increases, and our ability to consider empathic goals becomes more difficult.

Dix, T. (1992). Parenting on Behalf of the Child. In I. Siegel (Ed.), *Parental Belief Systems: The Psychological Consequences for Children.* Hillsdale, NJ: Lawrence Erlbaum Associates, pp. 319–346.

16. Thompson, R. A., Labile, D. J., and Ontai, L. L. (2003). Early Understandings of Emotion, Morality, and Self: Developing a Working Model. *Advances in Child Development and Behavior*, 31, 137–171. This research is discussed in Chapter 6.

17. See Lewis, C. C. (1981). The Effects of Parental Firm Control: A Reinterpretation of Findings. *Psychological Bulletin*, 90(3), 547–563.

18. Throughout this book, I will discuss research that supports these conclusions. For the benefits of valuing a child's emotions on children's friendships and academic achievement, see Gottman, J. M., Katz, L., and Hooven, C. (1997).

19. Damon, W. (2008). *The Path to Purpose.* New York: The Free Press.

Chapter 3

1. Neuroscientist Jaak Panksepp has presented a similar perspective on emotional health in childhood. Panksepp explains, "Positive emotional systems appear to operate as attractors that capture cognitive spaces, leading to their broadening, cultivation, and development. Negative emotions tend to constrain cognitive activities to more narrow and obsessive channels" (p. 132). He believes that "*As a general principle, the larger the sphere of influence of the positive emotions, the more likely is the child to become a productive and happy member of society*" (p. 143, italics added). Panksepp, J. (2001). The Long-Term Psychobiological Consequences of Infant Emotions: Prescriptions for the Twenty-First Century. *Infant Mental Health Journal*, 22(1–2), 132–173.

2. See Wyman, P. A., Cowen, E. L., Work, W. C., and Kerley, J. H. (1993). The Role of Children's Future Expectations in Self-System Functioning and Adjustment to Life Stress: A Prospective Study of Urban At-Risk Children. *Development and Psychopathology*, 5, 649–661; Werner, E. (1995). Resilience in Development. *Current Directions in Psychological Science*, 4(3), 81–85; and Sroufe, L. A., Egeland, B., Carlson, E. A., and Collins, W. A. (2005). *The Development of the Person*. New York: The Guilford Press.

3. See Seligman, M. E. P. (1995); Goldstein, S., and Brooks, R. B. (Eds.) (2006). *Handbook of Resilience in Children*. New York: Springer; and Lester, M., Masten, A., and McEwan, B. (Eds.) (2006). Resilience in Children. *Annals of the New York Academy of Sciences*, 1094, 83–104.

The concept of psychological immunity comes from Horton, P., Gewirtz, H., and Kreutter, K. J. (Eds.) (1988). *The Solace Paradigm: An Eclectic Search for Psychological Immunity*. Madison, CT: International Universities Press.

4. For the possible effects of prolonged stress on children's cognitive development, see Evans, G. W., and Schamberg, M. A. (2009). Childhood Poverty, Chronic Stress, and Adult Working Memory. *Proceedings of the National Academy of Sciences*, 106(15), 6545–6549. For the damaging neurological effects of prolonged stress in adults, see Sapolsky, R. (1996). Why Stress Is Bad for Your Brain. *Science*, 273, 749–750; and Kramer, P. (2005). *Against Depression*. New York: Viking Press.

5. In his classic work, *Persuasion and Healing*, psychiatrist Jerome Frank proposed that demoralization was the common characteristic of patients seeking psychotherapy, irrespective of the patient's specific symptoms and diagnosis. Frank's understanding of the syndrome of demoralization applies, in many respects, to children as well. What Frank proposed with respect to adult patients is also true of children: That a core feeling of demoralization, often silent or actively denied, and expressed in many different forms, is at the heart of what troubles most children. Frank, J. D., and Frank, J. B. (1961/1991). *Persuasion and Healing* (3rd ed.). Baltimore: The Johns Hopkins University Press.

6. Children, of course, do not feel discouraged at every moment or in every aspect of their lives. Even the most withdrawn child will continue to try and find some good feeling about himself, some place where he can experience a sense of acceptance and of pride. Because they are less able to sustain effort, however, demoralized children are likely to seek pride and acceptance in activities that provide an *immediate* good feeling—a

good feeling that does not have to be earned or worked for. For some children, video games have this appeal and, in adolescence, this is the appeal of risk taking, antisocial behavior, and substance abuse.

7. Or, at some later time, displaced against more vulnerable others, in bullying; or against groups of others, in bigotry.

8. Children with an impulsive temperament are at much higher risk for the development of defiant thoughts and behaviors. These children are not only more impulsive in their behavior; they are also more emotionally reactive—they become more quickly angry and have more difficulty learning to inhibit their angry and defiant responses. This quality of temperament therefore places great demands on the emotional maturity of parents and teachers, who are more likely to react harshly to the child's behavior, setting in motion the common, vicious cycle of angry interactions.

9. There are many definitions and many kinds of support that we provide for our children. In a study by psychologists Gregory Petit, John Bates, and Kenneth Dodge, four elements of supportive parenting were studied: parents' warmth, calm discussion in disciplinary encounters, interest and involvement in children's peer contacts, and proactive teaching of social skills. These positive parenting practices—not simply the absence of harsh parenting—assessed when children were entering kindergarten, were associated with better behavioral adjustment, peer relations, and academic performance, both in kindergarten and in the sixth grade. Supportive parenting was also able to partially offset the effects of stressful family circumstances. The authors suggest that supportive parenting "may serve as a protective factor against the risks associated with certain types of family adversity." Petit, G., Bates, J., and Dodge, K. (1997). Supportive Parenting, Ecological Context, and Children's Adjustment: A Seven-Year Longitudinal Study. *Child Development*, 68(5), 908–923, p. 918.

Chapter 4

1. I have taken the word *positiveness* from a 1993 research study by Jean Dumas and Peter LaFreniere. In their observations of preschool children and their mothers, Dumas and LaFreniere found that mothers of the most socially competent children (in contrast to children who were rated by their teachers as anxious, aggressive, or average in their social skills) showed higher levels of positiveness (laughter, helping, approving, and affectionate behaviors) and more frequent expressions

of positive feelings (for example, words of endearment and affectionate gestures) in their interactions with their children. The authors report, "Whenever competent children behaved positively, their mothers were likely to immediately reciprocate positively" (p. 1750).

These mothers, of course, were not *always* positive with their children. When mothers were more positive with their children, however, children were more likely to respond to, rather than ignore, their mothers' expressions of *disapproval.* Dumas, J. E., and LaFreniere, P. (1993). Mother-Child Relationships as Sources of Support or Stress: A Comparison of Competent, Average, Aggressive, and Anxious Dyads. *Child Development*, 64, 1732–1754.

There is now a substantial body of developmental and clinical research that supports and extends these observations of preschool children. Almost all empirically validated programs to reduce oppositional behavior in young children now include increased positiveness—in the form of more child-directed interactive play, more expressions of enthusiasm, or more frequent statements of appreciation and praise—as an essential component. See Kazdin, A. (2005). *Parent Management Training.* New York: Oxford University Press; Webster-Stratton, C., and Reid. M. J. (2003). The Incredible Years Parents, Teachers, and Children Training Series: A Multifaceted Treatment Approach for Young Children With Conduct Problems. In E. A. Kazdin and J. R. Weisz (Eds.), *Evidence-Based Psychotherapies for Children and Adolescents.* New York: The Guilford Press, pp. 224–240; and Brinkmeyer, M., and Eyberg, S. (2003). Parent-Child Interaction Therapy for Oppositional Children. In E. A. Kazdin and J. R. Weisz (Eds.), *Evidence-Based Psychotherapies for Children and Adolescents.* New York: The Guilford Press, pp. 204–223.

2. Emde, R. (1991). Positive Emotions for Psychoanalytic Theory: Surprises From Infancy Research and New Directions. *Journal of the American Psychoanalytic Association*, 39, 3–44.

3. Osofsky, J. (1995). Applied Psychoanalysis: Research With Infants and Adolescents at High Risk Informs Psychoanalysis. In T. Shapiro and R. Emde (Eds.), *Research in Psychoanalysis: Process, Development, and Outcome.* Madison, CT: International Universities Press, pp. 193–207, at p. 196.

4. For an artistic rendition of positive affect sharing, see Van Gogh's painting *First Steps.*

5. The psychoanalyst Heinz Kohut called this, simply, "the participation of others in these good feelings." Kohut taught what Freud, in his pessimism, had overlooked: that children want and need these joyful responses. Elson, M. (Ed.) (1987). *The Kohut Seminars*. New York: W. W. Norton.

6. Schore, A. (1994).

7. Fredrickson, B. (2001).

Lyubomirsky, S., King, L., and Diener, E. (2005). The Benefits of Frequent Positive Affect: Does Happiness Lead to Success? *Psychological Bulletin*, 131(6), 803–855. Lyubomirsky et al. present a review of research on positive emotions and arrive at this conclusion: Not only does success make people happy, but "positive affect engenders success."

8. Seligman, M. (2002), p. 28.

9. In my experience, it is not uncommon for parents to report immediate improvement in a child's mood and behavior when, as child therapists, we have done nothing else than respond to the child's interests and engage with her in animated play. In interviewing children hospitalized for severe aggressive behavior and emotional dyscontrol, I have also regularly observed that even deeply suspicious and angry children respond favorably to this form of affirming responsiveness and often, unexpectedly, open up.

10. I am not alone, of course, in making this recommendation, and I am not alone in reporting positive results. See, especially, Marston, S. (1990). *The Magic of Encouragement: Nurturing Your Child's Self Esteem*. New York: William Morrow and Company; and Covey, S. (1997). *The 7 Habits of Highly Effective Families*. New York: St. Martin's Griffin.

11. Child psychiatrist Stanley Greenspan and his colleagues have created a therapeutic program for children with special needs, called Floor Time, which serves as a model for this kind of parent–child interaction. In the Floor Time program, parents are instructed in how to create longer and longer play sequences, or "circles" of interaction, with their children. Floor Time procedures, developed for children with severe deficits in social engagement, are helpful for all children.

The following passage from Greenspan's book, *The Growth of the Mind*, illustrates the Floor Time method. Greenspan describes his work with a 2-year-old autistic girl. I will quote extensively from Greenspan's report:

> This . . . girl neither spoke nor made any response to those around her, but would spend hours staring into space, rubbing persistently at a patch on the carpet. We saw in her abnormal repetition, however, not only a symptom of her autism, but a sign of *interest* and *motivation* (italics added)—at least involving that little spot of pile. Perhaps it could serve as an opening wedge for emotional connection and, later, learning.

This is a creative and enormously therapeutic insight—that this child's autistic symptoms were an expression of interest and motivation; that is, this little girl *liked* rubbing the carpet, she *wanted* to do this. This understanding is not apparent, certainly not self-evident, if we focus on the child's behavior as a symptom, a deficit in communication and social engagement. Continuing with Greenspan's report:

> We had the girl's mother place her hand next to hers, right on the favorite stretch of floor. The girl pushed it away, but the mother gently put it back. Again she pushed, again the hand returned. A cat and mouse game ensued and by the *third* day of this rudimentary interaction, the girl was *smiling* (italics added) while pushing her mother's hand away. From this tiny beginning grew an emotional connection, a relationship, and then thoughts and words. From pushing away an obstructing hand to seeking out that hand and then offering flirtatious grins and giggles, the child progressed to using gestures in a reciprocal non-verbal dialogue. When she began repeatedly flinging herself at her mother, the therapist recognized that this behavior gave her sensory pleasure. He instructed the mother to whinny like a horse each time her daughter lunged at her. Soon she was whinnying too, imitating her mother . . . Over time, mother and child pretended to be neighing horses, mooing cows, barking dogs . . . It wasn't long before stuffed bunnies were fighting and hugging . . . At age seven, this girl has a range of age-appropriate emotions, warm friendships and a lively

imagination. She argues as well as her lawyer father, and scores in the low superior IQ range. (p. 17)

Greenspan, S. (1997). *The Growth of the Mind and the Endangered Origins of Intelligence.* Reading, MA: Addison-Wesley. See also Greenspan, S., and Wieder, S. (1998). *The Child With Special Needs.* Reading, MA: Perseus Books; Greenspan, S., and Wieder, S. (1997). Developmental Patterns and Outcomes in Infants and Children With Disorders of Relating and Communicating: A Chart Review of 200 Cases of Children With Autistic Spectrum Diagnoses. *Journal of Developmental and Learning Disorders*, 1, 87–143.

12. Wachtel, E. (2001). The Language of Becoming: Helping Children Change How They Think About Themselves. *Family Process*, 40(4), 369–383.

Chapter 5

1. John Gottman and his colleagues, for example, report evidence of the harmful effects of parental criticism on all aspects of a child's development—on a child's academic achievement, peer relationships, and physiology, including increased production of stress-related hormones that are potentially damaging to brain development. In these studies of parent–child communication, the parental behavior most directly related to measurable physiological stress in children was derogation or mockery, especially by fathers. See Gottman, J. M. (1997). *The Heart of Parenting*. New York: Simon & Schuster; and Gottman, J. M., Katz, L., and Hooven, C. (1997).

In a review of research, Bernadette Bullock and Thomas Dishion note that "Critical attitudes are associated with a broad range of psychological disorders . . . there is significant empirical support for the link between high levels of parent critical attitudes and child and adolescent externalizing disorders . . . Collectively, . . . findings suggest that children and adolescents with behavior problems are more likely to reside in homes in which their parents express criticism and negative affect toward them." Bullock, B. M., and Dishion, T. J. (2007). Family Processes and Adolescent Problem Behavior: Integrating Relationship Narratives Into Understanding Development and Change. *Journal of the American Academy of Child and Adolescent Psychiatry,* 2007, 46(3), p. 397.

In a 12-year follow-up of families who received The Incredible Years family treatment program, Carolyn Webster-Stratton reports that a mother's level of criticism and a father's use of praise were important predictors of these children's adjustment in adolescence. In a separate evaluation of a child-focused Incredible Years program, children whose parents continued to use high levels of criticism (and physical spankings) derived the least benefit from this treatment. See Webster-Stratton, C., and Reid. M. J. (2003). The Incredible Years Parents, Teachers, and Children Training Series: A Multifaceted Treatment Approach for Young Children With Conduct Problems. In E. A. Kazdin and J. R. Weisz (Eds.), *Evidence-Based Psychotherapies for Children and Adolescents*. New York: The Guilford Press, pp. 224–240.

See also Alloy et al. on the role of parental criticism in the vulnerability to depression in late adolescence. Alloy, L., Abramson, L., Tashman, N., Berreddi, D., Hogan, M., Whitehouse, W., Crossfield, A., and Morocco, A. (2001). Developmental Origins of Cognitive Vulnerability to Depression: Parenting, Cognitive, and Inferential Feedback Styles of Parents of Individuals at High and Low Cognitive Risk for Depression. *Cognitive Therapy and Research*, 25(4), 397–423.

2. Gottman, J. M. (1994). *What Predicts Divorce? The Relationship Between Marital Processes and Marital Outcomes*. Hillsdale, NJ: Lawrence Erlbaum Associates; Kazdin, A. (2005). *Parent Management Training*. New York: Oxford University Press.

3. Agassi, A. (2009). *Open: An Autobiography*. New York: Vintage Books.

4. The importance of "I-messages" (instead of "You-messages") was emphasized by Thomas Gordon in *Parent Effectiveness Training*.

5. There is one important exception to this rule: Children who are being bullied, at school or on the playground, have the right to fight back. At home, they need our complete support.

6. Damon, W. (1988). *The Moral Child*. New York: The Free Press.

Chapter 6

1. I present a brief review of this theory and research in Barish, K. (2009). *Emotions in Child Psychotherapy: An Integrative Framework*. New York: Oxford University Press, pp. 45–48. See also Graziano et al. (2007); Keenan, K. (2000); and Bradley, S. (2000).

2. The research of John Gottman and his colleagues on emotional communication in families offers compelling support for the importance of emotion regulation in healthy child development and has profound implications for how we, as parents, can foster the development of our children's social maturity.

Gottman described a style of communication and interaction with children he labeled "emotion coaching." Parents who use emotion coaching value emotions. They more often acknowledge and talk with their children about feelings, and they encourage the expression of anger and sadness by their children. In contrast, non-emotion-coaching parents—although they are not bad parents—are more often dismissive or derogatory toward their children's expressions of emotion.

Gottman and his colleagues found that children of emotion-coaching parents had better academic achievement, more successful peer relationships, and lower levels of stress hormones. In contrast, parental "derogation"—expressions of criticism, mockery, and contempt (especially by fathers)—was strongly associated with poor outcomes for children.

Based on these results, Gottman suggests that a child's ability to regulate her emotions, especially her ability to inhibit excessive expressions of negative emotions (for example, aggression, whining, and oppositional behavior) is the essential skill on which the development of other social skills depends.

A parent's coaching of a child's emotions leads, first, to improved physiological regulation. Lower physiological arousal then allows children to listen to what another child (or their teacher) is saying and to engage in joint problem solving. The child is therefore more successful, both in school and in her peer relationships. See Gottman, J. M., Katz, L., and Hooven, C. (1997).

3. In addition to the research discussed in this chapter, see also, Berk, L., E, Mann, T. D., and Ogan, A. T. (2006). Make-Believe Play: Wellspring for Development of Self-Regulation. In D. G. Singer, R. M. Golinkoff, and K. Hirsh-Pasek (Eds.) *Play = Learning: How Play Motivates and Enhances Children's Cognitive and Social-Emotional Growth*. New York: Oxford University Press, pp. 74–100.

4. Panksepp, J. (1998). Panksepp presents evidence to support the hypothesis that, among the many functions and benefits of play, in most mammalian species, play

> . . . may allow young animals to be effectively assimilated into the structures of their society. This requires knowing who they can bully and who can bully them. One must also identify individuals with whom one can develop cooperative relationships and those whom one should avoid. Play probably allows animals to develop effective courting skills and parenting skills, as well as increasing their effectiveness in various aspects of aggression, including knowledge of how to accept defeat gracefully. (p. 280)

5. Panksepp, J. (2001).

6. Parpal, M., and Maccoby, E. E. (1985). Maternal Responsiveness and Subsequent Child Compliance. *Child Development,* 56, 1326–1334. Parpal and Maccoby interpret these results (along with the results of previous studies) to support a "reciprocity" theory of behavioral compliance—the idea that even very young children are more likely to comply with their parents' requests when parents have complied with their child's requests. Their concise conclusion is worth noting and has significant implications for our understanding of children's social development: "Although we do not question the likelihood that Skinnerian processes can bring about changes in children's immediate compliance under some conditions, our results point to an entirely different set of processes. The 'responsive parenting' manipulation employed here did not involve reinforcing children for compliance, or giving them negative feedback for noncompliance" (p. 1332).

7. Bronson, P., and Merryman, A. (2009); Blair, C., and Diamond, A. (2008).

8. Bronson, P., and Merryman, A. (2009), pp. 168–169.

9. Psychologists Judy Dunn and Jane Brown, in their observations of patterns of communication between parents and young children, note that joking and teasing emerge very early in both parent–child and in sibling relationships. Teasing by children was clearly evident in these interactions at 24 months of age. "The essence of teasing is provoking an emotional reaction in another, and the delight of children in their success is all too evident, even in their second year" (p. 102). Dunn and Brown suggest that "a plausible case can surely be made that such interchanges are important to learning the acceptable limits of insult,

criticism, or expression of dislike in a significant emotional relationship" (p. 101). My clinical experience supports this hypothesis. Teasing occurs frequently in therapeutic play with children. And, as Dunn and Brown observe, a child's pleasure in teasing us—hiding, laughing at our errors, even playful cheating—is "all too evident." Dunn, J., and Brown, J. (1991). Relationships, Talk About Feelings, and the Development of Affect Regulation in Early Childhood. In J. Garber and K. A. Dodge (Eds.), *The Development of Emotion Regulation and Dysregulation*. Cambridge, UK: Cambridge University Press, pp. 89–108.

10. Psychoanalysis, although often characterized unfavorably, in both academia and in the public media, has taught this important lesson: Moral development depends on a child's identification with—her desire to be like—an admired parent or parent substitute. Admired adults become an inner reference that a child consults about what is right and what is wrong. In healthy development, doing the right thing becomes a source of inner pride.

11. For the best cinematic example I know of, recall the look on the faces of Scout and Jem as Atticus talks with them, or as he delivers his summation to the jury in *To Kill a Mockingbird*.

12. The psychoanalyst Heinz Kohut proposed that children's early idealizations of their parents are transformed, over time, through a process he called "optimal disillusionment" into our capacity, as adults, for commitment to guiding ideals. Kohut, I believe, identified a profound developmental truth: that, despite inevitable disillusionments, as parents, we should remain, in some way and to some degree, admired or respected, and that the preservation of ideals in some form is essential to emotional health. See Kohut, H. (1966). Forms and Transformation of Narcissism. In P. Ornstein (Ed.), *The Search for the Self: Selected Writings of Heinz Kohut: 1950–1978*. Madison, CT: International Universities Press, 1978, pp. 427–460. (Originally published in *Journal of the American Psychoanalytic Association*, 14, 243–272.) See also Elson, M. (1987).

13. Developmental psychologists have been able to observe this in infancy. If an infant is placed on a "visual cliff" or if a toy robot is placed in her crib, the child will look at her parent's face, to see if it is safe to explore. Robert Emde and his colleagues, who first studied this phenomenon, refer to the child's behavior as "social referencing."

Emde quickly appreciated, however, the more general significance of these observations. He defined social referencing in this way: when "an individual of any age encountering a situation of uncertainty looks to a significant other person for an emotional signal in order to resolve the uncertainty and to regulate behavior accordingly." Emde, R. (1991), p. 13.

14. Seligman, M. (2002).

15. Piliavin, J. A. (2003). Doing Well by Doing Good: Benefits for the Benefactor. In C. L. M. Keyes and J. Haidt (Eds.), *Flourishing: Positive Psychology and the Life Well-Lived*. Washington, DC: APA Press, pp. 227–247.

16. Dunn, E. W., Aknin, L. B., and Norton, M. I. (2008). Spending Money on Others Promotes Happiness. *Science,* 319, 1687–1688. Dunn et al. ask, if even $5 of prosocial spending can make us happier, why don't people make these small changes in their behavior? The answer, based on interviews of subjects in this research, is that we don't believe it's true: More subjects believed that personal spending, rather than prosocial spending, would make them happier.

17. This belief includes a corollary assumption: that children will behave badly, that they will challenge or defy adult authority, when it "works"—when they are able to avoid facing the consequences of their actions, when they have learned that they can "get away with it" (or, at least, that they have a good chance of getting away with it). Psychologist Russell Barkley, for example, a leading expert on attention-deficit/hyperactivity disorder (ADHD), compares the child's behavior to that of a gambler, who needs only an occasional win to reinforce his gambling habit. Children, in this view, also need only an occasional "win" (that is, avoiding punishment) to reinforce their tantrums and defiant behavior. Barkley, R., and Benton, C. (1998). *Your Defiant Child*. New York: The Guilford Press. The gambler analogy, however, is a narrow and misleading understanding of children's motivation and behavior.

18. Maccoby, E. E. (2007). Historical Overview of Socialization Theory and Research. In J. E. Grusec and P. D. Hastings (Eds.), *Handbook of Socialization: Theory and Research*. New York: The Guilford Press.

19. There is now an extensive literature, of both theory and research, on the development of prosocial behavior in young children. In this book of advice, I cannot review all of this research and do justice to the

complexity of the issues involved. I will present, instead, some ideas and conclusions from research studies that are often overlooked in how we think about our children's moral development—ideas that are especially relevant to our daily concerns and the choices we face as parents.

20. Emotion discourse, Thompson writes, "puts a human face on cooperation and compliance." He concludes that, "children in relationships with high amounts of shared positivity, and whose mothers made frequent references to other people's feelings, are higher in conscience." Thompson, R. A., Labile, D. J., and Ontai, L. L. (2003).

21. Eiesenberg, N., and Mussen, P. (1989). *The Roots of Prosocial Behavior in Children*. Cambridge, UK: Cambridge University Press. (See, especially, pp. 66–94; quote is from pp. 74–75.)

Chapter 7

1. Damon, W. (2008).

2. I recommend, especially, Stephanie Marston's excellent book, *The Magic of Encouragement*. Some of Marston's ideas, presented in a language of promoting children's self-esteem and a child's sense of "specialness," might elicit a chorus of criticism from contemporary parent advisors. Marston's recommendations, however, which transformed her own family life from one of conflict and exhaustion to one of pleasure and joy, are not overly permissive. Marston's message of encouragement and her recommendations to parents, recommendations that are also discussed in this book—on the importance of play and developing common interests; on focusing on a child's strengths; on expressing appreciation; on praising a child's effort and "support for each step along the way"; on expressing confidence; on avoiding "the sledgehammer of criticism"; on planning rather than reacting; on proactive, assertive discipline; and her recognition that parents also have needs—remain valid and important (see Marston, S., 1990).

3. Dweck, C. (2006), p. 193.

4. Synchrony games are similar to our first "conversations" with infants. When children begin to make speech sounds, we instinctively imitate these sounds, then expand them, changing their inflection and rhythm, to create a playful dialogue.

In his important book, *The Interpersonal World of the Infant*, psychiatrist Daniel Stern described another form of playful interaction between parents and infants he called "affect attunement." Affect attunement is different from simple imitation of a child's behavior. For example, when a baby shakes a rattle, a parent may shake her whole body, imitating the motion of the rattle. Stern believes that our attunement to the child's *affect* (in this example, her excitement) creates for the infant the experience of a shared state of mind. When parents are instructed to respond to their infant in a *mis*attuned way—to shake too quickly, for example, or too slowly—infants notice this mismatch and stop what they are doing. Stern, D. (1985). *The Interpersonal World of the Infant*. New York: Basic Books.

5. Balter, L. (1989). *Who's in Control?* New York: Poseidon Press.

6. See Fraiberg, S. (1959). *The Magic Years.* New York: Simon and Shuster.

7. Grossman, O. *The Genius of George Gershwin*. Audiotape Lecture presented for One Day University, 2010.

8. The report continues, "Compared to teens who have frequent family dinners (five to seven per week), those who have infrequent family dinners (fewer than three per week) are: twice as likely to use tobacco or marijuana; and more than one and a half times likelier to use alcohol. Teens who have infrequent dinners are likelier to say people at the table are talking or texting on cell phones or using other devices at the table such as Blackberries, laptops or Game Boys. Teens in households where dinners are infrequent and . . . distractions are present at the table are: three times likelier to use marijuana and tobacco; and two and a half times likelier to use alcohol. Compared to teens who have five to seven family dinners per week, those who have fewer than three family dinners per week are more than twice as likely to say it's hard to talk to their mothers and fathers about personal things" (p. ii). The National Center on Addiction and Substance Abuse at Columbia University (September 2009). The Importance of Family Dinners V.

9. Fivush, R., Bohanek, J. G., and Duke, M. *The Intergenerational Self: Subjective Perspective and Family History.* Emory Center for Myth and Ritual in American Life, Working Paper No. 44, November 2005. See also Duke, M. P., Lazarus, A., and Fivush, R. (2008). Knowledge of Family History as a Clinically Useful Index of Psychological Well-Being and Prognosis: A Brief Report. *Psychotherapy Theory, Research, Practice, Training*, 45(2), 268–272.

10. Parenting advisor Julie Ross calls these "love tickets." Ross, J. (2008). *How to Hug a Porcupine.* New York: McGraw Hill.

11. Diamond, A., and Amso, D. (2008) Contributions of Neuroscience to Our Understanding of Cognitive Development. *Current Directions in Psychological Science*, 17(2), 136–141. Diamond and Amso conclude,

"Thus, besides 'simple touch' being able to calm our jitters and lift our spirits, the right kind of touch regularly enough early in life can improve cognitive development, brain development, bodily health throughout life, and gene expression" (p. 139).

12. Thompson, J. (2009). *Positive Sports Parenting.* Portola Valley, CA: Balance Sports Publishing, LLC.

13. Gottman, J. M., Katz, L., and Hooven, C. (1997).

14. Johnston, J. (1993). Family Transitions and Children's Functioning: The Case of Parental Conflict and Divorce. In Cowan, P. A., Field, D., Skolnick A., and Swanson, G. E. (Eds.), *Family, Self, and Society.* New York: Lawrence Erlbaum, pp. 197–234.

15. Davies, P., and Cummings, E. M. (1994). Marital Conflict and Child Adjustment: An Emotional Security Hypothesis. *Psychological Bulletin*, 116(3), p. 397; Cummings, E. M., and Davies, P. (1995). The Impact of Parents on Their Children: An Emotional Security Perspective. *Annals of Child Development*, 10, 167–208.

Chapter 8

1. For some problems, a formal assessment of a child's attention, language, or motor skills is necessary. This is especially true when children struggle with their homework.

2. Levine, M. (2003). *The Myth of Laziness.* New York: Simon and Schuster.

3. Kazdin, A. (2008). *The Kazdin Method for Parenting the Defiant Child.* Boston: Houghton Mifflin.

4. The idea of a "home base" for children who have frequent meltdowns comes from Myles, B. S., and Southwick, J. (1999). *Asperger Syndrome and Difficult Moments.* Shawnee Mission, KS: Autism Asperger Publishing Co. See also Baker, J. (2008). *No More Meltdowns.* Arlington, TX: Future Horizons.

5. Parens, H. (1987). *Aggression in Our Children.* Northvale, NJ: Jason Aronson.

Chapter 9

1. Leman, K. (2008). *Have a New Kid by Friday.* Grand Rapids, MI: Baker Publishing Group.

2. Overly solicitous (Leman, K., 2008); overconcerned to "soothe each minor unpleasant feeling" and have turned our homes into "little democracies" (Mogel, W., 2001); "determine their own upbringing" (Hymowitz, K., 1999).

3. Although there are some differences in these programs, there are also shared principles and shared procedures. The most important of these shared principles is increased positive interactions between parents and children and the judicious, even minimal, use of punishment as a disciplinary technique. See, especially, Kazdin, A. (2005, 2008); Brinkmeyer, M., and Eyberg, S. (2003); Webster-Stratton, C., and Reid, M. J. (2003).

4. Kazdin, A. (2008), p. 141.

5. Schreiber, J. (2011). Minimizing Power Struggles: Understanding, Respecting, and Responding to Your Child's Behavior. Available at http://www.jeanschreiber.com.

6. For a moving example of the dangers of consequences—how these techniques can cause rebellion and alienation when they become the central focus of a parent's efforts—see Peter Jensen's personal account of his relationship with his son. Jensen writes openly about the conflict caused by these methods—and how it was resolved, over time, by empathy and understanding. Hallowell, E.M., and Jensen, P. (2010). *Superparenting for ADD*. New York: Ballantine Books.

7. Alan Kazdin also makes this recommendation.

8. Phelan, T. W. (1995). *1-2-3 Magic: Effective Discipline for Children 2–12* (2nd ed.). Glen Ellyn, IL: Child Management, Inc. Phelan's approach to parent guidance, however, is, in many respects, directly contrary to my own. I recommend this technique only for use in circumscribed problematic situations (especially, fighting among siblings). Although Phelan recognizes the importance of shared fun and active listening, he believes that, in promoting healthy parent–child relationships, effective discipline comes first. (Phelan includes a chapter on active listening at the end, rather than at the beginning, of his book.) In my opinion, listening comes first and discipline is second. Counting to three is an adjunct, certainly not the essence, of good parenting, and the magic of encouragement is far more important than the magic of 1-2-3 (see Marston, S., 1990).

9. Coercive family interactions were described several decades ago by scientists studying families of children with severe behavior problems. These cycles begin when a child makes a demand or with his initial refusal to comply with his parent's commands. When he continues his demands or his refusal, his parents—now more angrily—repeat their requests. Over time, both parents and children become increasingly angry and threatening. Eventually, parents give in, and the child's tantrum or defiant behavior has been unwittingly "reinforced." He has learned that his defiance works. (And his parents have also been reinforced, in their capitulation, by some momentary respite from their child's demands.) Or a child may eventually give up and comply in response to his parent's angry threats. In this case, parents come to believe that "he only listens when I yell at him"—and therefore yell more often.

In a recent revision of coercion theory, Granic and Patterson have expanded their understanding of these unhealthy interactions. They note that the harmful effects of coercive cycles go far beyond reinforcing a child's defiant behavior. Coercive interactions are also characterized by emotion dysregulation, by frequent expressions of anger and contempt, and by increasingly inflexible patterns of behavior on the part of both parents and children. These cycles then "escalate": Parents and children develop generalized negative attributions and expectations of each other, and more subtle provocations (for example, a sigh or rolling of the eyes) now trigger angry reactions. Granic, I., and Patterson, G. R. (2006). Toward a Comprehensive Model of Antisocial Development: A Dynamic Systems Approach. *Psychological Review*, 113(1), 101–131.

10. Kazdin, A. (2008), p. 75. Again, in the language of behaviorism, this is called "shaping." We could equally call it "appreciation."

11. Kazdin notes, for example, that, as children enter their preteen and teenage years, principles of behavior management (for example, reinforcement and shaping) increasingly give way to dialogue, negotiation, and compromise.

Chapter 10

1. Mel Levine's book, *The Myth of Laziness* (2003), should be required reading for all families (and therapists) who struggle with this problem.

2. In my experience, the identification of learning disorders is often delayed for several years because schools—and clinicians—have made

the *assumption* that a child's resistance to schoolwork was based on emotional problems. During this time, families have pursued unsuccessful psychotherapy, parent–child conflict over schoolwork has remained unabated, and children have failed to receive appropriate academic accommodations and remedial support, increasing their demoralization and anger. It is essential to accurately diagnose learning disorders—to identify, as early as possible, a child's areas of academic difficulty—and to provide appropriate remedial intervention.

3. These principles also apply to the homework and procrastination problems of middle school and high school students. Solving the homework problems of older students, however, is often more difficult; it takes more time to work through the demoralization—and bad habits—these teenagers have developed.

4. Cooper, H. (2001). *The Battle Over Homework* (2nd ed.). Thousand Oaks, CA: Corwin Press, p. 65.

5. The 2003 Brown Center Report on American Education: How Well Are American Students Learning? The Brookings Institution. October, 2003, Vol. 1, Number 4. Available at http://www.brookings.edu.

Chapter 11

1. Yanof, J. A. (1996). Language, Communication and Transference in Child Analysis. *Journal of the American Psychoanalytic Association*, 44(1), p. 91.

Chapter 12

1. Damon, W. (2008), p. 130.

2. See "Coach's Philosophy" at http://www.coachcarter.com

Chapter 13

1. Greene, R., and Ablon, J. S. (2006). *Treating Explosive Kids.* New York: The Guilford Press.

2. Eyberg, S. M. (1999). *Parent-Child Interaction Therapy Treatment Manual.* Gainesville, FL: University of Florida.

3. Myles and Southwick call this the child's "home base." Myles, B. S., and Southwick, J. (1999). See also Baker, J. (2008).

4. See Kazdin, A. (2005, 2008).

5. Turecki, S. (2010). Managing the Difficult Child: Effective Strategies for Professionals and Parents. Lecture presented at Young Child Expo, New York City, April 9, 2010.

6. Alan Kazdin also makes this recommendation (Kazdin, A., 2008, p. 78).

7. This advice comes from Glasser and Easley (1998). Glasser and Easley refer to this as Time Out/Reset. Glasser, H., and Easley, J. (1998). *Transforming the Difficult Child: The Nurtured Heart Approach.* Nashville, TX: Vaughn Printing.

8. This advice comes from Alan Kazdin's research. See Kazdin, A. (2008).

Chapter 14

1. I have taken this phrase from Jaak Panksepp's discussion of the role of play in social development. See Panksepp, J. (1998), p. 280.

2. This behavior—the cheating syndrome—was described in a classic essay published 40 years ago by child psychiatrist John Meeks and can still be observed with unchanged regularity (Meeks, J., 1970. Children Who Cheat at Games. *Journal of the American Academy of Child Psychiatry*, 9, 157–170). Meeks notes that, in normal development, school-age children are serious about game play and about the rules of the game. They regard the game—as they should—as an opportunity to test and improve their skill. Preschool children have not yet reached this stage of development. Their play, in contrast, is characterized by a mood of triumph and "naïve invincibility."

3. Harter, S. (1988). Developmental and Dynamic Changes in the Nature of the Self-Concept: Implications for Child Psychotherapy. In S. Shirk (Ed.), *Cognitive Development and Child Psychotherapy.* New York: Plenum Press, p. 122.

4. I need to make note of one additional aspect of this dimension of children's emotional development. I have found that difficulties of this kind—the problem of cheating and other problems of moral socialization—are more common among children who lack a supportive relationship with their fathers. A child's father may be absent (or emotionally absent), or angry and critical, or himself unable to accept defeat gracefully. This aspect of a child's emotional life is difficult to observe; children will only occasionally tell us about it. But a child's learning to

play by the rules may depend, more than anything else, on his knowledge that the adults he admires, and whose approval remains important to him, also play by the rules. In the absence of this guiding influence, a child's adherence to rules is likely to remain tenuous, too easily overtaken by the emotion of the moment.

Chapter 15

1. Dahl, R. E. (1999). The Consequences of Insufficient Sleep for Adolescents: Links Between Sleep and Emotion Regulation. *PhiDeltaKappan*, 80(5), 354–359.

2. Bronson, P., and Merryman, A. (2009), pp. 36–37.

3. Anderson, C. A., Gentile, D. A., and Buckley, K. E. (2007). *Violent Video Game Effects on Children and Adolescents: Theory, Research, and Public Policy.* New York: Oxford University Press. See also Anderson, C. A., Berkowitz, L., Donnerstein, E., Huesmann, L. R., Johnson, J. D., Linz, D., Malamuth, N. M., and Wartella, E. (2003). The Influence of Media Violence on Youth. *Psychological Science in the Public Interest*, 4(3), 81–110; American Academy of Pediatrics Joint Statement on the Impact of Entertainment Violence on Children Congressional Public Health Summit. Available at http://www.aap.org/advocacy/releases/jstmtevc.htm; and American Psychological Association Resolution on Violence in Video Games and Interactive Media. Available at http://www.apa.org/about/governance/council/policy/interactiv-media.pdf.

4. Singer, D. G., and Singer, J. L. (2005). *Imagination and Play in the Electronic Age*. Cambridge, MA: Harvard University Press.

5. Singer, D. G., and Singer, J. L. (2005).

6. The processing speed of the original Sony *PlayStation* was 350,000 polygons per second. The processing speed of *PlayStation3* is 275 million polygons per second; the processing speed of Xbox360 is 500 million polygons per second.

7. Anderson, C. A., Gentile, D. A., and Buckley, K. E. (2007).

FURTHER READING

There are many good books that offer sound advice to parents on different problems of raising our children. The following list, briefly annotated, is not in any way exhaustive. I have selected the books and articles that have been most influential in my own work with children and families, and that I recommend most often to parents.

CLASSICS

Ginott, H. (1965). *Between Parent and Child*. New York: Three Rivers Press.

The standard for parenting advice was set, many years ago, by Haim Ginott's, *Between Parent and Child*. It is still difficult to improve on Ginott's understanding of children and his wise recommendations.

Gottman, J. M. (1997). *The Heart of Parenting*. New York: Simon & Schuster.

In this book, John Gottman presents his important research on family communication and "emotion coaching."

Greenspan, S. (1993). *Playground Politics*. Reading, MA: Addison-Wesley

Greenspan, S. (1995). *The Challenging Child*. Reading, MA: Addison-Wesley.

Stanley Greenspan made many important contributions to child psychiatry and to helping parents raise happy and emotionally healthy children. These parenting books are based on Greenspan's work with children with autistic spectrum disorders and other developmental challenges. See also Brazelton, T. B., and Greenspan, S. I. (2000). *The Irreducible Needs of Children*. Cambridge, MA: Da Capo Press.

Greenspan, S. (1997). *The Growth of the Mind and the Endangered Origins of Intelligence*. Reading, MA: Addison-Wesley.

In *The Growth of the Mind*, Greenspan describes insights gained from his work with autistic children, and he extends his ideas about child development to other social problems.

Marston, S. (1990). *The Magic of Encouragement: Nurturing Your Child's Self Esteem*. New York: William Morrow and Company.

Psychologist and family therapist Stephanie Marston published this very helpful book when my children were young. Her message of encouragement remains valid and important.

Russert, T. (2006). *Wisdom of Our Fathers*. New York: Random House.

A moving collection of correspondence Russert received following the publication of his memoir of his relationship with his father.

SPECIAL TOPICS

Anxiety and Depression

Chansky, T. (2000). *Freeing Your Child From Obsessive-Compulsive Disorder*. New York: Random House.

Chansky, T. (2004). *Freeing Your Child From Anxiety*. Cambridge, MA: Da Capo Press.

Chansky, T. (2008). *Freeing Your Child From Negative Thinking*. Cambridge, MA: Da Capo Press.

Helpful techniques, based on cognitive-behavioral research, for helping children with these problems.

Seligman, M. (1995). *The Optimistic Child*. Boston: Houghton Mifflin.

In this book, Martin Seligman describes a successful program for reducing pessimism and strengthening psychological immunity in elementary school children.

Attention-Deficit Disorder (ADD)

Hallowell, E. M., and Jensen, P. (2010). *Superparenting for ADD*. New York: Ballantine Books.

ADD experts Ned Hallowell and Peter Jensen write about the need to appreciate the "gifts," not just the deficits and difficulties, of living with ADD.

Hallowell, E. M., and Ratey, J. J. (2005). *Delivered From Distraction: Getting the Most Out of Life With Attention Deficit Disorder.* New York: Ballantine Books.

Essential information and recent research on ADD.

Bullying

Blow, C. (2009). Two Little Boys. *New York Times*, April 24, 2009.

A journalist's report of research documenting an increase in suicidal thoughts among children who have been subjected to bullying—and a tribute to two young victims—that deserves to be read by all parents.

Children's Books

Here are three of my favorites:

Keller, H. (1984). *Geraldine's Blanket*. New York: Greenwillow Books.

Long, E. R. (1987) *Gone Fishing*. Boston: Houghton Mifflin Harcourt.

A brief picture book that beautifully captures the feelings of a young boy in his relationship with his father.

Miller, M. (1987). *My Grandmother's Cookie Jar*. Los Angeles: Price, Stern, Sloan, Inc.

Defiant Behavior

Kazdin, A. (2008). *The Kazdin Method for Parenting the Defiant Child.* Boston: Houghton Mifflin.

The Kazdin Method is the state-of-the-art program for resolving problems of defiant behavior.

Schreiber, J. (2011). *Minimizing Power Struggles: Understanding, Respecting, and Responding to Your Child's Behavior*. Available at http://www.jeanschreiber.com.

Excellent tips on avoiding power struggles with young children from an experienced early childhood educator.

History

Hulbert, A. (2003). *Raising America.* New York: Vintage Books.

A history of parenting advice (and the personalities of the advice givers) over the course of the 20th century.

Hrdy, S. B. (2009). *Mothers and Others*. Cambridge, MA: Harvard University Press.

An eminent anthropologist's ideas on the role of communal child rearing in human evolution.

Homework

Cooper, H. (2001). *The Battle Over Homework* (2nd ed.). Thousand Oaks, CA: Corwin Press.

Learning

Levine, M. (2002). *A Mind at a Time*. New York: Simon and Shuster.

Levine, M. (2003). *The Myth of Laziness*. New York: Simon and Shuster.

Shaywitz, S. (2003). *Overcoming Dyslexia*. New York: Knopf.

Media Violence

Singer, D. G., and Singer, J. L. (2005). *Imagination and Play in the Electronic Age*. Cambridge, MA: Harvard University Press.

Motivation and Purpose

Damon, W. (2008). *The Path to Purpose*. New York: The Free Press.

In this book, William Damon reports the results of his study of the development of a sense of purpose in adolescents and young adults.

Dweck, C. (2006) *Mindset: The New Psychology of Success*. New York: Random House.

An important new idea for parents and teachers, based on extensive research.

Psychiatric Medicine

Kalikow, K. (2006). *Your Child in the Balance*. New York: CDS Books.

A thoughtful discussion by an experienced child psychiatrist on whether and when to prescribe psychiatric medicine to children.

Sports

Thompson, J. (2009). *Positive Sports Parenting*. Portola Valley, CA: Balance Sports Publishing, LLC.

Must-read advice for all parents of children involved in organized sports.

Tantrums

Baker, J. (2008). *No More Meltdowns*. Arlington, TX: Future Horizons.

Greene, R. W. (1998). *The Explosive Child*. New York: Harper Collins.

INDEX